CONTENTS

Chapter One: Prying eyes

Chapter Two: Identity cards

Chapter Three: Freedom of information

Introduction

Private Lives is the thirtieth volume in the series:
Issues For The Nineties. The aim of this series is to
offer up-to-date information about important issues
in our world.

Private Lives looks at civil liberties with particular
reference to CCTV, identity cards, computer records
and freedom of information. The information comes
from a wide variety of sources and includes:

Government reports and statistics
Newspaper reports and features
Magazine articles and surveys
Literature from lobby groups
and charitable organisations.

It is hoped that, as you read about the many aspects
of the issues explored in this book, you will critically
evaluate the information presented. It is important
that you decide whether you are being presented
with facts or opinions. Does the writer give a biased
or an unbiased report? If an opinion is being expressed,
do you agree with the writer?

Private Lives offers a useful starting-point for those
who need convenient access to information about
the many issues involved. However, it is only a
starting-point. At the back of the book is a list of
organisations which you may want to contact for
further information.

*****

Who's snooping on you?

Most of us prefer to keep certain details about our lives private – the amount of money we have in the bank, for example. In theory, gaining access to such details without permission is impossible – and illegal. But with computerisation of records now commonplace, a person with the right know-how can find out in a matter of hours . . .

Finding such a person is as easy as opening the Yellow Pages at 'Detective Agencies', and looking for those that offer 'Personal Histories' or 'Background Research'. To see if it really is that simple, I chose an agency at random, and said I needed background information about someone, but knew only her name, telephone number and date of birth. I was told this was all that was necessary, and that obtaining the information would cost £500. The name I asked to be investigated was my own. Four days later, I was given a report.

Home address

Finding out where I live took 'minutes'. Markus Marku of Legal Solutions is a commercial investigator who does not carry out any of these procedures, but is familiar with the processes involved. An address, he explains, is easily obtained from BT, even if the person is ex-directory. 'An agency will have a contact at BT who simply looks up the name and phone number from the database. They'll be paid around £75 for it.'

A BT spokesman comments: 'A person can be given a telephone number by Directory Enquiries if they know the name and address, but not if the number is ex-directory. No-one should be given an address on the strength of knowing a telephone number. If a customer address is obtained through a BT employee, then it is a breach of our employment regulations and is a disciplinary offence. We would appreciate any information that would allow us to pursue this internally.'

By Anna Walker

Bank balance

My bank account number was traced and I was told my exact balance – to the penny. Getting this information, says Markus Marku, usually involves a contact with access to the bank's database. 'There is a network of people who can tap into this information almost instantly and do so for payment. Obviously, this is illegal so they tend to be very transient and disappear after a while to avoid detection.'

Medical history

The report included the juiciest titbits from my medical past – prescriptions, operations and other treatments.

The Patient's Charter states: 'You have the right to know that everyone working in the NHS is under a legal duty to keep your records confidential.'

However, Markus Marku says that computerisation of medical records has made them accessible, as many surgeries are linked up to local health-authority systems.

Non-computerised records are trickier. An investigator may ring a doctor's surgery direct, and impersonate, say, a hospital consultant, requesting medical information. But by far the most common method is to use a contact inside the profession.

Credit references

A court judgement for non-payment of poll tax appeared in my report, along with when it was ordered, and by which court. According to Markus Marku, this would have been on my credit file. This is a legitimately held record of credit worthiness, used by credit-givers to assess who is and isn't a good risk. Credit cards, credit limit and outstanding debts, plus mortgage details, may also be held.

Any information on the file should be used only when you are applying for credit, and given solely to the organisation to which you're applying. However, Markus Marku points out that simply *sounding* like a credit organisation – asking the right questions, using the right phraseology

IT'S NOT ME THAT WANTS TO KNOW THE COMPUTERISED DETAILS OF MY PRIVATE LIFE —IT'S MY WIFE!

– will be enough to gain access to a file. Computer access is given to businesses that regularly carry out credit transactions. Agencies have inside contacts who access these files.

Who wants to know?

'I am asked to check out a lot of CVs,' the man at my agency informed me. 'I'll find out if a person really does earn as much as they say, or if they have the degree they claim to have. I'm often asked to check out a person's bank balance. Sometimes it's as easy as going to their home and looking in the dustbin. Lots of people throw away statements, and if you know their bank details, someone can access their file. I've also had men who want to find out things about a prospective wife.'

Does the law help?

All information held on computer is protected by the Data Protection Act 1984. Under this Act, any organisation that holds information about you on a database – the police, BT, your doctor's surgery, your bank – can reveal information to registered individuals only. Those who reveal information to unregistered individuals are committing an offence and can be prosecuted and fined, says Neil Marshall, Compliance Manager at the Data Protection Register. 'We are aware that there may be individuals within organisations who give out information to unauthorised persons – either for money, or because they know the person, or because they have been deceived.'

Last year, the Data Protection Act was amended by the Criminal Justice Act. It has become an offence to procure information from a data user when you are not registered to receive it. Previously, only the person giving out the information could be prosecuted.

The law becomes more woolly when information received is not on computer. 'There have been attempts to prosecute for this, using laws such as the ancient one that says it is an offence, generally, to do something counter to someone else's interest. None has been successful,' says Neil Marshall. 'It is, however, an offence to impersonate a police officer, if information was obtained that way, but it isn't an offence to impersonate a member of the medical profession.'

So what can be done? The Data Protection Register is now in the process of supplying information to certain organisations that use databases, to make them more aware of possible abuses of the system, and to give them advice on ways to make information more secure. And, as Neil Marshall points out, 'We should start to see the first prosecutions under the amended Data Protection Act coming through very soon.'

Depending on the outcome, this may deter potential abusers.

Detective agencies that are members of the Association of British Investigators and the Institute of Professional Investigators undertake to abide by the Data Protection Act, and will only search information and investigate using methods that comply with the Act.

If you are concerned about who has access to information about you, contact the Data Protection Register, tel: 01625 545745.

What personal details are you prepared to give to a company if requested?

Source: Dataculture, The Henley Centre/DMA

Caught – by the long lens of the law

A growing number of cities are employing television monitors to help control crime. But are they a threat to personal liberty?

By Oliver James

Tony is fighting with another man. He throws him to the ground, steadies himself, takes aim with his left foot and lets fly. All this is seen on a monitor at the City Centre TV (CCTV) control centre in King's Lynn, Norfolk.

The victim did not press charges. But the police decided to prosecute because the severity of the incident had been captured on film.

Tony, 30, initially denied any violence but, when told that his actions had been recorded, immediately confessed. He was found guilty and given a stiff sentence, solely because of what the police had been able to see on screen.

There are now over 220 CCTV schemes planned or operating in Britain, and 95 per cent of local authorities are considering adopting the idea. It looks as though these covert eyes of the law could succeed in changing the criminal justice system by producing more prosecutions, more convictions and more informed sentencing. And their very presence is thought to be a deterrent to crime.

However, the growth of CCTV is not without its pitfalls. Andrew Puddephatt, director of Charter 88 which campaigns for greater democracy, claims there is an urgent need for legislation to protect the public from abuses.

'There is nothing to prevent private companies setting up wholly unregulated schemes, or the filming of people for political reasons, or for pornographic purposes,' he said.

In one city (not King's Lynn), operators are known to have made a tape of members of the public in intimate clinches. The pictures are explicit and of good quality, and the participants easily identifiable.

This tape has been widely copied and distributed as pornography; there is growing concern that such tapes could be compiled at other centres.

Recently, the Home Office set up three scientific studies to evaluate CCTV's effectiveness. Spokesman Robert Smith is convinced there will be no case to answer. 'We're not concerned about sceptics and criminologists. All the cities involved will tell you that it works and the people on the street have less fear of crime.'

Individual schemes support this view, pointing to dramatic decreases in several categories of crime, especially car theft. Following the introduction of CCTV to council car parks in King's Lynn thefts dropped from 207 in 1991 to 10 in 1992 – in 1994 there were none. But is there an unforeseen price? One King's Lynn criminal solicitor believes there is. 'On balance, CCTV is a good idea, but there is a difficulty about who owns the video material.

'In one case, we suspected there was footage which might incriminate the police. When we demanded it from the crown prosecutors, they claimed to have returned it to the police – who said it was council property. The council said it belonged to the police. We still have not seen it.'

This is an area that would seem to need legislation, otherwise material that embarrasses the prosecution might be in danger of getting 'lost' or of being withheld.

The 'staff notes and procedures' at the King's Lynn CCTV control room show why. Officers are instructed: 'The prime purpose of the King's Lynn CCTV system is to deter crime and to provide quality evidence to aid detection and conviction . . . police may 'seize' tapes for their own use at their own discretion.'

By contrast: 'Requests from any source other than the police should always be politely refused.' Despite its successes, Andrew Puddephatt maintains that CCTV is a major threat to civil liberties: 'All-pervasive surveillance is now foreseeable. It is going to give future authorities tremendous powers and tremendous opportunities to exert social control over us.' But the blank eye of the lens could also gain respect as a guardian of modern communities, taking the place of the busy-bodies of close-knit streets and villages who once kept crime at bay.

Its most positive use is well illustrated by an incident in Darlington, broadcast last night on Channel 4 in *When the Fighting Starts*, a programme about violent assaults captured on CCTV. A notoriously violent youth is shown punching a man outside a nightclub. Later, he claims that he was provoked, but the video evidence does not bear him out. In cases such as this, not only does CCTV make it easier to get sound convictions, but it can also make it clear who was to blame.

But frequently CCTV proves that everyone has a different version of the same event. 'Usually nobody is right about what happened,' the King's Lynn lawyer said.

'Seeing the video often shows that neither prosecution nor defence accounts are correct. It's not necessarily because anyone is lying. Often it's simply that memory is fickle; we see what we want to see.'

Someone to watch over you

Video cameras that can read your number plate or identify your face are just two of the systems police are investigating for the next century, writes Matthew May

Cities using closed-circuit television cameras to monitor their streets have reported massive drops in such crimes as muggings and assaults. The public is impressed, and the Government has stumped up £5 million to help towns buy the equipment. Despite all this, though, CCTV could soon be overtaken by more sophisticated technology.

The equipment in use today is 'dumb'. It needs an operator, which means it is expensive, and its recordings of events require time-consuming analysis to be of use. Most important, the faces on the screen are anonymous. Virtual Interactive Policing (VIP), a new system under consideration, could change all that.

The system, based on advanced neural network principles that emulate how the human brain works, uses software linked to remote video cameras to enable officers to scan a crowd or street and automatically cross-match the faces against a database of offenders. A variety of factors, from classifying by ethnic group to the distances between different features on a face, are analysed. Commercial systems in development promise to produce accurate matches within seconds from databases containing thousands of images.

Next week the Police Foundation and the Forensic Science Service are expected to announce an initiative to put facial recognition systems on a firm statistical foundation. This is necessary for the results of facial matching systems to be admissible in court in the same way that fingerprint and DNA analyses are today. Prototype systems are being used in court, but only by getting expert witnesses to vouch for their accuracy.

> ## To be effective the system requires access to a large database of faces. Such a database does not exist – yet

'It's difficult if the courts are faced with a facial image of a robbery in progress and the subject picked up claims the photo is not of him or her,' says Barrie Irving, the director of the Police Foundation.'

The Police Foundation is also involved in a project to bring together police records and databases of images from private security sources, including images from bank and building society security cameras.

'There are all these mugshots in police hands, and a huge database captured from security cameras. As town centre and shopping mall cameras are used more and more, archives are being built up,' says Irving. 'But if the police are sent one picture from a bank raid, it's very difficult to see if they've got a match.'

Building a bridge between the private systems and police records will make it possible to search for an individual's involvement in thousands of recorded incidents. The system can also look for multiple appearances by the same individual: since the date, time and location of each raid are also stored, 'it is possible to generate criminal intelligence about someone even if you don't know who they are', says Irving.

He adds that the experimental system is available for detectives to 'come and play'. Once such a system has proven its worth, the applications for it are endless. 'The onward development of this technology is for sifting people at immigration or customs.'

To be effective the system requires access to a large database of faces. Such a database does not exist – yet. The Government has plans for a new driving licence that will include a digitised image of the driver's face: a potential database of 30 million faces.

To the police, such technology is seen as a boon. The advantages of VIP – the ability to patrol without the presence of a police officer – is the effect it has on resources. According to the Metropolitan Police's department of technology, it is looking at VIP as one answer to what it describes as an 'unrelenting conflict between finite police resources and the widespread public demand for improved crime control'.

But for civil libertarians, it has worrying implications. 'Of course the police must have all the tools they need in the fight against crime, but we are concerned about the question of accountability,' said a spokesman for Liberty. 'There is a balance to be found.'

Future possibilities include linking to image-enhancement software that, for example, could artificially age pictures of wanted people when up-to-date pictures are not available.

Image-analysis software can also be used to read and recognise a vehicle's number plate. A hidden camera scans a section of road. When a car enters its field of vision, the software quickly identifies the number plate and then, using pattern-matching techniques, reads the characters.

Since it, too, is based on a neural network, it can be 'trained' to recognise a pattern so that numbers that are dirty or pictured from an angle can still be recognised. The whole process, from entering the field to a final output, takes 0.25 seconds.

Customs and Excise officials are interested in the system for border monitoring. It can be 'taught' to recognise foreign plates and linked to international databases. The police have talked about using it in the 'Ring of Steel' around the City of London. By fixing the camera just ahead of the checkpoints, suspect cars can be intercepted as they approach.

Video also lends itself to automated surveillance. A system called Astraguard 'watches' an area and can be programmed to respond either to movement, such as an intruder, or lack of movement, such as a car parked in a sensitive area for too long. It triggers video recorders that capture the event on a timed log, and can raise alarms.

In theory, Astraguard could be linked to the recognition software, enabling police, for example, to build up a list of everyone who entered a house under surveillance, or the number plate of every vehicle that passed through a sensitive area.

The greater use of video is only one of the areas police are investigating. Large investment is being made in the use of computers, in support roles (such as processing offender data) and in operational use, such as the Police National Computer (PNC), which gives all of the country's forces access to serious crime information, including murder, rape, blackmail and kidnapping.

PNC links are currently found only in stations. But mobile data links in cars are being considered, giving patrolling officers immediate access to its information.

The use of Personal Digital Assistants (PDAs), such as the Apple Newton, is currently being evaluated by some forces to replace the traditional notebook. PDAs can be loaded with the most up-to-date information on suspects, stolen cars and burglaries.

Geographic information systems are being used to pinpoint crime patterns while fingerprints can now be taken by laser and immediately checked against police records in seconds.

By the early 2000s, when all these disparate systems could be fully integrated and working with each other, the familiar face of the bobby may no longer be Jack Warner or Inspector Morse, but a camera mounted on a pole.

© *The Telegraph plc London, 1996*

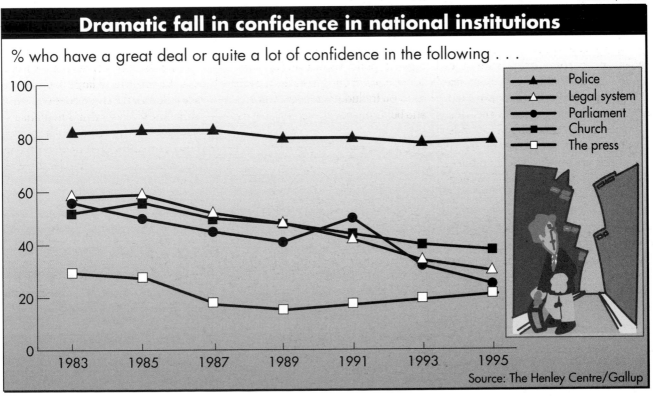

Dramatic fall in confidence in national institutions

% who have a great deal or quite a lot of confidence in the following . . .

Police
Legal system
Parliament
Church
The press

Source: The Henley Centre/Gallup

The surveillance society

Closed Circuit Television (CCTV) is everywhere: in our streets, public transport, housing schemes, shops, hospitals and football grounds . . . even cash card machines and fire engines. But for whose benefit?

By Andrew Puddephatt

There are over 220 CCTV schemes in operation or planned, and an astonishing 95 per cent of local authorities have established schemes or are considering them. We should be asking why.

Police, local authorities and private companies make great claims for video surveillance: it helps to catch criminals (for example, the Bulger case and the Harrods bombing); to deter crime, to monitor large demonstrations (all of which are now routinely filmed); to pursue disciplinary action against staff; to provide public reassurance; and even save the costs associated with trials, because it may encourage defendants to plead guilty.

There's no detailed monitoring or research to support these claims about video surveillance, and yet people seem to want it. A 1992 Home Office report said that 80 to 90 per cent of people welcome the introduction of cameras. A poll conducted in Glasgow showed that less than one third of the people felt safe in the streets at night, that 66 per cent of people felt that CCTV would make them safer, and 40 per cent were more likely to visit the town centre if CCTV was installed.

Public perception is at the heart of the debates about CCTV. The reason for the growth of video surveillance is the public fear of crime, and the manipulation and promotion of that fear by an avid market. In Glasgow, for example, crime had actually dropped by 26 per cent before the introduction of CCTV cameras.

Despite this, the survey showed public anxiety at a high level. Public perception of crime is out of sync with the reality of crime, so that even if crime falls, or the real impact of crime isn't addressed by new technology, the public fear creates a climate conducive to the introduction of ID cards or CCTV systems.

But public perceptions may change if people feel themselves to be the targets of CCTV in circumstances where no criminal activity is contemplated. At Brightlingsea, for example, where the police have been filming demonstrators, residents have voiced concerns about the legality of the film and how it will be used.

Security makes money: £300 million a year, according to *The Times* newspaper. The British Security Industry Association (BSIA) says the market has doubled since 1989, and estimates that there are 150,000 professionally-installed camera systems in Britain, with 500 more added each week. The Government has introduced a new 'challenge' scheme, offering £2 million for which local authorities can bid, in partnership with the police and the private sector, to install CCTV systems.

Soon there will be a wide surveillance network in this country

But no research has yet established the effectiveness of CCTV systems. Three Home Office research projects are currently looking at CCTV. One of these is a study by the Police Research Group, to find 'the characteristics of schemes' that control crime and help the police, which seems odd research to be carrying out after so many schemes have already been introduced.

It's a striking combination: the absence of any authoritative research, and the large number of schemes already in existence. James May, of the British Retail Consortium, has said that: 'Whilst there is some evidence that crime has been reduced in some towns which first introduced systems, there is no evidence to date that retail crime costs or level of sales have improved.'

So there's little research, and there's no regulation – there are no statutory enforceable guidelines governing the use of CCTV. Home Office guidelines are now being issued to set out local codes of practice for CCTV systems – covering named local officials in charge of CCTV systems, secure control rooms and police checks on proposed operators, for example – but these guidelines have no legal force. There is nothing to prohibit the filming and recording of people for political, trade union or sexual activity, and nothing to prevent private companies setting up wholly unregulated schemes.

It's interesting to note that there's little use of CCTV elsewhere in Europe, and we're regarded with amused fascination by our European partners for rushing to install systems wholesale.

Soon there will be a wide surveillance network in this country, though there's no hard evidence of its effectiveness and there are no legal controls. We're seeing policy on crime driven by a marketed, manipulated, public fear of crime – and we've seen in the United States that there are no logical ends to the punitive systems that evolve in such a climate.

All-pervasive surveillance is now foreseeable. It is going to give future authorities tremendous powers, and tremendous opportunities to exert social control over us all. Are we really going to drift towards that without public debate? and without legislation? © *Agenda June, 1995*

Why CCTV?

A cure looking for an illness

Plans for CCTV are often triggered by the installation of a system in a nearby town, or simply by word of mouth. Too often CCTV is perceived as the 'cure' before clearly identifying the problems with which it is supposed to deal!

You should not assume that CCTV will solve all your problems. Superintendent Peter Durham puts the installation of CCTV in Newcastle in the context of other efforts in the city to deal with crime. He indicates how a strategic approach, incorporating CCTV as one element, may have reduced the numbers of recorded crime from 13,500 to 9,000 over a two year period.

Case study – Newcastle City Centre CCTV system

'On the 4th December 1992, a 16 camera closed circuit television system with microwave transmission was launched within the city centre environment of Newcastle. The control room is based in the confines of the police station and is monitored by police officials. The area of Newcastle city centre encompasses 1.25 miles square and a huge concentration of retail, commerce and leisure.

1991 saw this police area record some 13,500 crimes and yet following the introduction of a revised style of pro-active policing, which included the introduction of a Door Supervisors' Registration Scheme and a Pubwatch Scheme, the area saw a reduction on that total of some 4,500 crimes to the end of 1993. The introduction of CCTV during the whole period of 1993 has in that year been a contributory factor to the reduction of crime by some 2,381 offences. A significant number of arrests have been effected with the pro-active use of CCTV and, to date, all cases involving the use of CCTV

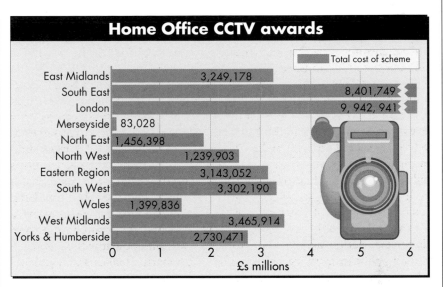

Home Office CCTV awards

Region	Total cost of scheme (£s millions)
East Midlands	3,249,178
South East	8,401,749
London	9,942,941
Merseyside	83,028
North East	1,456,398
North West	1,239,903
Eastern Region	3,143,052
South West	3,302,190
Wales	1,399,836
West Midlands	3,465,914
Yorks & Humberside	2,730,471

have appeared at court on a "guilty" plea basis.

There is no doubt that the effects of closed circuit television had a massive bearing on reductions of crime and disorder in the area. The true success of CCTV however must be linked to a strategy of pro-active policing and other positive initiatives which are inextricably linked to the use of CCTV. If such a strategy is in place, then the successes currently enjoyed here in Newcastle will be achieved, but no-one can expect to derive such success by the use of closed circuit television alone.'

Peter Durham
Superintendent, Newcastle Division,
Northumbria Police

Though of course cameras are unable to act in quite the same way as police officers, in relation to the scheme in Liverpool, Superintendent Howard Parry has expressed the view that, 'this scheme is equivalent of 20 police officers on duty 24 hours a day taking notes, with no meal breaks, holidays and taking no sick leave.'

Action

Your first move should be to form a multi-agency working party compromising all interested parties. Consider involving:

- Police, including police solicitors
- Relevant local authorities, including County and District Councils, Metropolitan Boroughs, London Boroughs
- Local representative of the Crown Prosecution Service
- Crime Prevention Panels
- Representatives of retailers and other city centre businesses (post offices, banks, building societies, pubs, clubs and restaurants, betting shops, offices, bus companies, railway stations, taxi firms etc.)
- Car parking operators
- Town Centre Manager
- Chamber of Commerce
- A representative of the media, for example the editor of the local newspaper.

What is the problem?

It is vital, but not easy, to start with a 'clean sheet'. CCTV must be put to one side at this stage and the problems identified. You should not assume that CCTV will resolve the problems – and then attempt to make it do so. Do not begin with CCTV as your cure, and then look for problems it might solve! Start with the problems and identify the best solutions which may *include* CCTV!

Conduct a brainstorming session. Run it non-judgementally, starting by identifying possible problems in your town. The second part of the brainstorming sifts the ideas, and the objective is to end up with a concise but exhaustive list of all issues relating to security.

Possible problems relate to:

- Vandalism, theft from and theft of motor vehicles in streets and car parks
- Shoplifting
- Vandalism
- Drug taking/dealing
- Drunkenness
- Burglary
- Fear of crime amongst shoppers/ workers/visitors
- Terrorist attack
- Racial harassment
- Sexual harassment
- Robbery/ram raiding/smash and grab
- Fuel drive off
- Lost/missing children
- Violent attacks
- Pickpocketing
- Groups loitering
- Disorderly behaviour.

After brainstorming, it is important that you check out your hunches by collecting hard evidence. Get data from the police, from retailers, from the council and from other interested parties. In some cases it may be worth asking the public, especially about fear of crime. Find out exactly where the problems are in your town. Are there particular times of day when problems are especially serious? Are there days of the week or times of the year when problems surface? You need a precise, well defined statement of the problems to be addressed before you can begin to think about appropriate solutions, including the installation of CCTV.

Case study

In one borough, a high rate of vandalism to cars was believed to be driving people from using the town centre. It was thought that CCTV would be the best solution. Further research revealed, however, that the damage was concentrated on particular days of the week. It then emerged that the problem appeared most commonly during one period of time on those days. Moreover, it was found that when the damage occurred, the cars had typically been parked in one small area. When this was investigated it turned out that the problem was not one of vandalism at all. Instead, the higher than normal rate of damage was caused by careless market traders when they set up early in the morning! The lesson is obvious. Town centre CCTV would have been an expensive non-solution. The problem needed an altogether different approach.

What are the possible resolutions?

Next, discuss and list all possible ways of dealing with the listed problems. Remember possible solutions like:

- Targeted improved lighting
- Business/Shop/City Watch schemes. (Do existing schemes work effectively?)
- Radio link
- Security guards/companies
- Security patrols
- Quick repair of damage
- Speedy removal of graffiti
- Wider aisles to prevent pick-pocketing in markets
- Altered police patrolling patterns
- Unobstructed views into and out of high street premises
- Barrier-entry car parks
- Improve natural surveillance
- Businesses in or overlooking car parks
- Creation of living space above shops
- Bye-laws about drinking on the streets
- Training for bar staff, shop staff etc. to show what they can do to reduce crime
- Nightclub doorman registration.

Is CCTV the best answer to the identified problems?

Will other suggested ideas provide cheaper and/or more effective answers? You may need to mix more than one idea, which might include CCTV.

How exactly might CCTV help deal with the problems?

CCTV does not, of course, automatically prevent crime. It is not like a physical barrier which is difficult to overcome, nor alone is it like a police officer or security guard who can immediately intervene. You need to think through how it is going to help reduce problems in your town, either on its own or in conjunction with other measures.

- The above is an extract from *CCTV Closed Circuit Television – Looking out for you*, produced by the Home Office. © *Home Office*

CCTV *used to spy on* employees

As employers attempt to crack ̄ ̄ ̄n high levels of crime, Stephen Overell reports on the ̄ ̄ ̄ ̄V in the workplace

Big Brother may be watching, but the workers seem to be turning a blind eye. Whether it takes the form of covert snooping or blatant surveillance, the use of closed-circuit television (CCTV) is becoming increasingly common.

After a five-year boom, CCTV is the fastest-growing sector of the security industry. The Federation of Small Businesses reports that almost one-quarter of British firms now have it and believe it is one of the most effective crime deterrents. Retailers spent £89.8 million on surveillance equipment last year in a bid to stop losses of £664 million from customer theft and a further £446 million stolen from tills by employees.

Beyond this figure, no one knows the extent of CCTV in the workplace because, unlike burglar alarms, surveillance systems do not have to be registered with the police. Perhaps the most reliable indicator is the increasing number of security firms offering to fit cameras into office clocks, plants and even mobile phones.

Camera surveillance is usually justified by the rising tide of workplace fraud, a problem that accounts for twice as many company failures as bad debt, according to the Society of Practitioners of Insolvency. Guy's hospital, for example, realised that mail was going missing from the post room last year, and covert cameras were fitted after consultation with the police. When hospital staff found out, the issue was taken up by their union. The cameras were subsequently removed, the theft ceased and an agreement requiring consultation before surveillance is now under negotiation.

But beyond crime, opinion is divided on the effect of CCTV in

th ̄ ̄ ̄ ̄ ̄ ̄ ̄ ̄s staff- ̄ ̄ ̄ ̄ ̄ ̄ ̄ ̄ ̄ ̄ ̄ ̄ ̄ and the ̄ ̄ ̄ ̄ ̄ ̄ dent trust ̄ ̄ ̄ ̄ ̄ ̄ ̄ ̄ployees do ̄ ̄ ̄ ̄ ̄ ̄ ̄ ̄ ing watched, accor ̄ ̄ ̄ ̄ ̄ ̄. 'People are used to c ̄ ̄ ̄ erywhere, but employers shou ̄ want to avoid surprising their employees with spy cameras,' said Mike Emmott, the institute's employee relations policy adviser.

Such advice is not without foundation. Liberty, the civil liberties watchdog, has examples of secret cameras being fitted to employees' rest areas in old people's homes, while senior managers in other organisations have had their conversations filmed in lifts. NTV, a firm that has made a small fortune from making videos from scenes captured on CCTV, has covert camera pictures of couples having sex in stationery cupboards when their employer had hoped to catch a pilferer. The law does not intrude because there is no right to privacy at work.

Firms that install these systems tend not to ask questions. Covert systems are often in demand for specific purposes. 'If there is a spate of equipment going missing, an employer is better off renting a system until it stops,' said Gareth Jones, managing director of First Associated Security Group. 'The rental market is huge.' However, a spokesman for Chiswick Security said that the use of CCTV 'to keep an eye on workers' was becoming more common.

Trade unions only object when surveillance is covert. For the shop workers' union Usdaw, cameras are a reasonable part of employment. 'Obviously it depends where it is placed, but we can't start shouting

about staff insecurity when one of the greatest deterrents to violence against staff is CCTV,' a union spokesman said.

A spokeswoman for Unison said: 'CCTV only becomes an issue if it is brought in without agreement. Staff should not be in situations of danger; that is bad management. But CCTV can help.'

For banking union Bifu, surveillance cameras benefit both employer and employee, provided they are used only for security. The Metropolitan Police has introduced CCTV to 'custody suites' to reassure groups concerned about police brutality.

Ray Evans, director of support services for Goodwill Associates, an independent CCTV consultancy, said less than 5 per cent of employees complain once a system is fitted. But he stressed the importance of understanding the nature of the problem the camera was supposed to solve. 'It can only ever be part of an answer,' he said.

The use of cameras to satisfy a Machiavellian boss is rare, according to Tony Makosinska, marketing manager of the British Security Industry Association. 'It is either to make people feel more secure or to deal with a specific problem such as theft,' he said. 'It is rarely of use in monitoring staff because the view of the camera is very narrow, although you do sometimes find them above tills.'

However, a new EU directive concerning the covert filming of someone without their consent is likely after October 1998. Big Brother may continue to watch, but the employee will at least know about it.

© People Management
April, 1996

Are you being scanned?

Electronic eavesdropping first hit the headlines with 'Squidgygate' but the growing army of scanner fans take an interest in us all

By Sean Blair

The royal family must curse the day they bought their first mobile phone. Over the past five years Charles, Diana and Philip have all had their intimate conversations splashed over the nation's tabloids – and there are rumours of the existence of other taped conversations kept under lock and key. But while they make the headlines such celebrity snoops are just the tip of the iceberg; there's plenty more to listen to out there.

We live in an invisible ocean of radio signals, from air traffic communications to radio ham broadcasts, satellite signals to taxi radios, police and military transmissions to baby-monitor intercoms. But while this traffic is invisible, it is definitely not inaccessible. For about £250 you can buy a radio scanner that makes the airwaves your oyster – and thousands of people have done just that.

Radio scanners – which are manufactured by such companies as Icom, AOR and Yupiteru – browse this ceaseless traffic, searching the entire frequency spectrum for signals then automatically honing in. They were invented as a means of tracking down ham radio signals, but, as use of the radio frequency spectrum has enlarged, so has the range of uses and the sophistication of scanners on the market.

Scanners have been coming into this country in sizeable numbers for the past eight years or so. Despite the impression given by the royal eavesdropping stories, owning a scanner is perfectly legal. It's what you do with it that can get you into trouble.

Scanning and the law
There are two separate areas of law that govern scanning. Listening in on mobile telephone calls is forbidden under the 1985 Interception of Communications Act – a conviction carries a £5000 fine or up to two years in prison. Eavesdropping on all other private radio signals – and 'private' includes everything from police frequencies to your dustmen's walkie-talkies – is outlawed by another, older piece of legislation, the 1949 Wireless and Telegraphy Act, under threat of a fine (also £5000) and confiscation of equipment, but no prison sentence.

So why are scanners available at all? The answer, according to the Department of Trade and Industry, is that they do have legitimate uses, including the receiving of licensed amateur 'ham' transmissions, citizens' band (CB) radio and for just listening to normal radio broadcasts

But is this really what scanner enthusiasts do for fun? A salesman in an electrical shop in London's Tottenham Court Road made it clear what the main attraction was for his clients. 'You're interested in scanners?' he began. 'So you want to listen in to mobile calls...' His voice dropped and he looked round cautiously as he outlined the eavesdropping pleasures to be had.

'You can hear it all with these scanners, all the mobile frequencies. It's in the evenings they really start to liven up, you know. I've heard some quite outrageous stuff.'

But while a bit of illicit eavesdropping may be tempting, snags soon become apparent with the mobile phone variety of scanner. For a start, you don't know what you're going to get: other people's phone calls can be pretty dull – discussing what train they're getting home, their next sales appointment, what colour dress they should buy. And what you hear often lasts only 15 to 30 seconds. If the caller is on the move, the signal moves from one 'cell' of the network to another, and changes frequencies as well. Specialised equipment can follow a call from one frequency to another,

Ten of the best spot frequencies

Freq.	Mode	Location	User
39.5000	NFM	Nationwide	Army tanks channel
76.9250	NFM	West Midlands	USAF base security
86.5000	NFM	...onwide	BNFL nuclear incident channel one
123.1000		...nd	Air mountain rescue
142.4000			Mir space station
157.6500	N...	...le	Fish... patrol boats
166.7000	NF...		...cret
169.2375	NFM		
259.9750	AM		
414.4875	NFM		...P...

Fourth... ...tory, ...narrow)

but its £20,000 price tag puts it well out of reach of the hobbyist.

In a few years, the entire cellular phone network should be beyond the average scanner's reach anyway, as the move from analogue to digital signals is completed. More than a million UK users – now including the royals – are on digital networks. Digital mobile calls are broadcast *en masse* via 'multiplexes': only the receiver's handset can pick out the one message aimed for it. If you pick up the right frequency with a standard scanner, all you hear is a noisy blast of overlapping signals, each composed of coded pulses rather than actual speech. Not that there's such a thing as total security: digital decoding programs are available, and the price is coming down.

The rest of the airwaves spectrum is charted in a publication called the UK Scanning Directory (now in its fourth edition). This lists more than 20,000 spot frequencies you can tune in to, from those used by the army in Northern Ireland and air-traffic control at Heathrow, to Swindon's Oasis leisure centre and the London Underground's Victoria Line.

It works too. Testing a hand-held scanner in Spymaster, a London surveillance shop, yielded exchanges from a secret service detachment of the US Embassy – right where the book said it would be – though a combination of static and code made the messages unintelligible.

...sher John Barnes wa... ...en the first edition came ... a colossal grey area. I studied it ...efore publishing, but in the back of my mind was the thought that we might be raided by the police. The government insinuates that it's wrong but it turns out that while it's illegal to listen to these frequencies, it's not illegal to list them.'

The directory, which Barnes says is superior to DTI and military publications, was contributed to by hundreds of scanner fans who he says range 'from QCs on down'.

The privacy market

While most users scan for fun, some are in it for money. As well as royal-tape sellers, there are scanner users who listen to the emergency services and sell journalists stories 'as they happen', or tip off insurance assessors when a building burns down.

'Scanner' – aka Robin Rimbaud, a DJ – samples mobile phone conversations. To stay on the right side of the law, he 'denatures' the voices so they can't be recognised. 'I can't deny there's a voyeuristic element, but the material also points to serious issues of personal communication.' Many of the samples highlight the poignant lack of communication between men and women.

As if having your personal life sold for entertainment weren't bad enough, government may have you taped for less amusing purposes. It was confirmed last year that a unit at RAF Digby, Lincolnshire, is licensed to eavesdrop on public phone networks and other army/intelligence agencies have the same powers.

British, French and German intelligence bodies have insisted that the EU downgrade the encryption code for the new 'global system for mobiles' (GSM) – to make it easier for them to listen in. Not only is Big Brother scanning you; he wants you to speak clearly too.

© Focus
June, 1996

Rise of the clone phone

Scanners can seriously damage your phone bill. Many of the 15,000 phones stolen in the UK each month are 'cloned' using scanners. After locking on to the signal from any mobile phone, crooks download the electronic serial number, then re-chip a stolen phone with these details.

Calls made on this 'clone phone' show up on the innocent phone user's bill. Businesses are the preferred target, as more calls go unnoticed. Vodafone has introduced a PIN to prevent cloning – the phone rings off if the number isn't transmitted. But the switch to digital networks, which are much harder to scan, should put an end to cloning.

ID cards – a solution looking for a problem

The government's range of options

The Camden Papers

In January 1995, some government documents found their way into the public domain via a filing cabinet in a junk shop in Camden; their authenticity was subsequently confirmed by civil servants. The papers describe proposals being discussed in May 1994.

A Cabinet committee studying the possible uses of card technology in a range of different government departments moved on to concentrate specifically on a national ID card scheme after Michael Howard suggested that there had been growing interest in the case for a national ID card. An internal government memorandum notes 'signs that the general public may find such a card more acceptable now than in the past,' adding that 'the time may now be ripe for a Government document to test opinion on the subject.' However, concerns are also expressed that an ID card scheme would be 'contrary to our deregulatory stance', and that reservations amongst chief police officers could 'cause presentational problems'.[1]

The Green Paper

The Green Paper outlines six options:[2]

1. **The status quo**: this isn't really an option – see 'photographic driving licences' below.
2. **Voluntary ID card**: a simple, voluntary national ID card as a travel card within Europe could be a replacement for the British Visitor's Passport. It would include name, nationality, date of birth, photograph and signature. It would be issued for

a period of 5 or 10 years by the Passport Agency. No legislation would be required to introduce the card, although some parliamentary approval would be needed to charge a fee. The costs are likely to be £10 to £15 per card.

3. **Photographic driving licences**: The DVLA is already going ahead with plans to introduce photos on driving licences, in order to comply with a European Union Directive. These will be introduced by July next year, although existing paper licences will continue to be valid for several years. As the paper acknowledges, if it were decided not to issue a separate ID card, the photographic driving licence would be used in many circumstances as a de facto ID card. No separate legislation would be required unless a voluntary non-driver's card were also introduced.

4. **Combined driving licence and ID card**: driving licences and ID cards could be combined into one card for some 36 million drivers.

5. **Multi-purpose government card**: such a card could be used more widely for identity, driving licences and the payment of state benefits. Such cards could also be developed and financed by the private sector, using smart card technology, and could be used for banking, payment in shops, and so on. A multi-function card would require legislation, and much further

consideration of the technical feasibility.

6. **A compulsory I-D card scheme**: this could use either a simple card or a multi-function 'smart card'. The Green Paper makes many claims for the benefits of a compulsory scheme in reducing illegal immigration, benefit and credit fraud, burglaries by bogus officials, and crime in general. Such claims stand up to little scrutiny. It could be made a criminal offence not to carry a card, and the police could be given powers to demand proof of identity without having to give a reason. However, the paper acknowledges that this might have a 'negative impact' on relations between the police and the public.[3]

The technology

As outlined in the introduction to this briefing, earlier announcements by the DVLA and the DSS, together with comments in the Green Paper, and in the 'Camden Papers', strongly suggest that a 'smart card' would be the preferred option.

However, the Green Paper outlines a number of possibilities:[4]

1 A basic card

A basic card made from paper or plastic can carry information printed on its surface. It can include a photograph and signature so that visual checks can be made of the card-holder. This type of card does not carry data in machine readable form.

2 A bar code

A bar code such as those used on items in shops can be printed on the surface of the card. The code can only be read by an optical scanner. The storage capacity can be increased if the bar coding is two dimensional.

The coding can include numbers, letters, a digitised photograph, personal identification data or any combination of these.

3 Optical character recognition

Optical characters can be added to the face of a card, allowing it to be machine readable by an Optical Character Recognition reader. The information is printed in a special format which can also be read visually.

4 Magnetic stripe card

A card can have the addition of a magnetic stripe, like those commonly used on credit cards. This can hold a limited range of information such as a digitised photograph. It can be updated using a suitable reader/writer device. It is often used in conjunction with a Personal Identification Number (PIN).

5 Optical card

This is a plastic card which can store a very large amount of data in optical form. Information in machine readable form is recorded by a laser which creates a pattern of tiny pits on the card's recording layer; these are digitally coded to represent numbers, graphics and characters. The information cannot be changed once it is written into a card.

6 A smart card

A smart card is essentially a very small computer microprocessor embedded in credit card sized pieces of plastic. The card is powered and activated through contact with or proximity to a reader/writer device – either through electrical contacts on the card or through radio-frequency linkage over a limited distance. The reader/writer enables data to be exchanged with any other computer system, and for the record carried by the card to be modified.

The microprocessor in the card executes instructions from the operating system and the applications programs to interpret and manipulate data. It's the microprocessor that makes the smart card 'smart', and enables it to carry out functions such as encryption of data and the alteration of existing records.

The best available technology at present provides a maximum memory capacity of 32KB. This is roughly equivalent to 3,000 words, a quarter of the length of this briefing.

The information stored in the card's memory can be structured into zones:
- completely inaccessible to the cardholder (secret zone)
- accessible only after a PIN, for example, has been entered (working zone)
- accessible though not changeable by the cardholder (open zone).

A contactless system would mean that it would be technically possible for a reader/writer device to read or alter information on a card without the knowledge or consent of the cardholder – e.g. while walking through a doorway.

The CCTA report (one of the 'Camden Papers') also mentions that a smart card system could be used to record the transactions conducted with the card, and thereby track the movements of the card holder. Although only a limited number of entries could be held on the card itself, a much higher number could be compiled by a central computer connected to the system.[5]

7 A hybrid card

This makes use of more than one type of technology, e.g. combining an integrated circuit chip with a watermark magnetic stripe.

Security and verification

The Green Paper identifies the need for a card to be secure against alteration, copying, fraud, theft and other forms of misuse. Plastic cards can be made secure by the addition of techniques such as PINs, holograms, watermarks, or data encryption. The suitability of each technique would depend on the type of card that was issued, the level of associated risk and the required levels of security.

Verification

A number of means are suggested by which the user of a 'smart card' can be validated. These involve the writer/reader device being linked to a means of biometric verification using a feature of the card-holder.

For a biometric to operate an individual must first provide an example of the particular characteristics that are to be used when verification is required. This process called enrolment allows the system to create a template of the characteristic such as a signature or fingerprint image. Once the template has been obtained it is used in the process of verification when comparing against a newly offered set of characteristics.

Signature and voice are examples of behavioural characteristics. As the Green Paper acknowledges, they cannot precisely be used to prevent an individual from assuming multiple identities, and so may need to be used in conjunction with documentation checks at the time of card issue and details of physical attributes. Possible unique physical characteristics which could be used include hand geometry, fingerprints, the pattern of the iris in the eye, the pattern of blood vessels on the retina, and the shape and contours of the ear.

Cost estimates

The Green Paper suggests that a compulsory scheme would cost over £600 million to introduce, or possibly more depending on the type of card chosen.[6] Given that large computer projects frequently have a bad history of development and implementation problems, sometimes with significant cost over-runs, this is likely to be a conservative estimate. The Green Paper gives no running costs, though earlier government estimates have put these at around £150 million a year. An internal government report suggests that under a voluntary scheme, charging individuals for cards would be an option, with the likely cost starting at £5.00.[7]

References:
1. Memorandum, Wakeham to Prime Minister, 25.5.94.
2. Identity Cards: a consultation document, CM 2879, HMSO, 1995 (pp 22-32).
3. Ibid (p 31).
4. Ibid (Annex A).
5. The Smartcard Report, CCTA, May 1994.
6. Identity Cards, plo.
7. The Smartcard Report.

● The above is an extract from ID – A solution looking for a problem, produced by Liberty. See page 39 for address details.

© Liberty
June, 1996

The consumer's need for identification

Information from the National Consumer Council

At present consumers have to provide identification in a number of situations. Some are statutory or at least compulsory requirements of public bodies. Under the Money Laundering Regulations a person wishing to open a bank or building society account can be required to provide proof of identity. The police can ask for evidence of identity where they believe a false identity is given by a person believed to have committed an offence. Evidence of identity is required when applying for a passport. Other requirements are a matter of practice, but are in effect compulsory. For example, banks and shops require proof of identity when cheques are cashed or used to pay for goods.

Consumers have to show entitlement when applying for state or local authority benefits. In some cases this will involve proving identity in some form. For example, when applying for child benefit, the parent has to prove that the child exists; forms are issued by the hospital in which a child is born. In other cases, what needs to be shown is that the applicant's circumstances are such that he/she is entitled to benefit. This might involve proof of incapacity for work, or evidence of income. In more simple cases, such as application for membership of a local authority library, consumers may need proof of residential status.

In cases where the applicant has first to prove entitlement, he/she is usually issued with a document which shows that this has been done. The document usually acts as proof of entitlement and proof of identity. Examples of this kind of document are benefit books or library cards. When using these, further proof of identity is not normally required. Possession is assumed to prove that the person holding the book or card

is the person entitled. If there were evidence that large numbers of people are using stolen benefit books, further proof of identity could be required before a benefit cheque could be cashed.

Other situations may arise where the government feels it necessary to require proof of identity where it is not required at present. In the Netherlands, for example, since the introduction of voluntary identity cards, proof of identity is required by statute when applying for a job.

Whether or not identity cards are introduced, consumers should know when and why they are obliged to identify themselves. The situations in which it is obligatory should be transparent and the means by which it can be achieved should be known. If consumers do not have this knowledge there will be occasions when they will not be able to get a

service, public or private, because they are not aware of the need to prove identity or because they do not know what will be accepted as proof.

How identity can be proved

At present where identity alone is an issue, it can be proved by:

- a third party confirming that the person is who he/she says he/she is (for example in passport applications);
- possession of a document which allows the person to whom it is presented to assume that the presenter is who he/she says he/she is (for example a cheque guarantee card indicates that the person presenting the cheque is also the holder of the bank account);
- showing one document or a combination of documents which confirm the presenter's name and address (for example a combination of a driver's licence and letters addressed to the presenter at his/her home address).

Although these methods of proving identity are common, they do not, in

fact, prove anything other than the fact that the person presenting them is in possession of the papers which claim to prove that he/she is who he/she says (except in the case of the passport application). Nevertheless, for most purposes other than those involving crime they are sufficient.

For many people these requirements are not onerous or impossible. People with stable life styles are able to produce this kind of identification. They can match the standard of proof required to the application being made.

Others, however, who live more on the margins of society, including those who live isolated lives in rural areas, who move frequently, who are homeless, who suffer mental health problems, may find the production of identification in the form currently accepted more difficult. If the introduction of identity cards is to benefit individuals, it must benefit all individuals or groups and not discriminate between them.

Benefits of identity cards for individuals

The green paper suggests that an identity card could be of benefit to an individual in several circumstances. It could be used as a travel document within Europe instead of a passport. It could be used by young persons or retired persons as proof of age. It could be used to show identity when opening a bank account. It could be used by retail customers who wish to hire goods, obtain credit or pay by cheque for an amount above the usual limit. It could contain emergency medical information or organ donor details. It could be used to show entitlement to certain benefits and services.

At present all these functions are performed separately by different forms of identification. Those who travel have a passport, although the simple form of British Visitors Passport is to be withdrawn, so all travellers will require a full passport. Young and old persons who have to prove their age can do so by presenting their birth certificate, student union card or their pension books. Evidence needed to open a bank account is provided by a

combination of different documents, as is proof of identity in retail or credit and hire transactions. Organ donors carry donor cards and can enter these details on their driving licence. Those who suffer from medical conditions can carry cards to alert those who might treat them. Entitlement to benefits is shown by possession of a benefit book.

These differing forms of identity require different levels of proof. Proving you are entitled to a passport requires considerably more evidence than proving you are entitled to a library card.

If the government decides to introduce a card which can replace all these different forms of identification, the proof of identity required to obtain one will have to be the same for all, and it will have to be the most stringent. There is a danger that it will become usual practice to ask for an identity card for any transaction. There is evidence from abroad that even if cards are not compulsory, voluntary cards rapidly become in effect compulsory. The effect could

be that those who want merely to join the library will have to offer the same standard of proof of identity as those who want to travel abroad.

The only way around this problem would be to make the identity card a multi-function card, with more or less information stored on the card according to the needs of the carrier. This would then raise the question of whether consumers are happy to have a large amount of personal information stored on a card which they cannot read. For most people their understanding of an identity card is probably a card which bears the person's name and address and perhaps photograph and date of birth. If a multi-function card becomes the key to services, consumers will need to know what is contained on them.

● The above is an extract from *Identity Cards – Response to the Home Office green paper*, published by the National Consumer Council. See page 39 for address details.

© *National Consumer Council June, 1996*

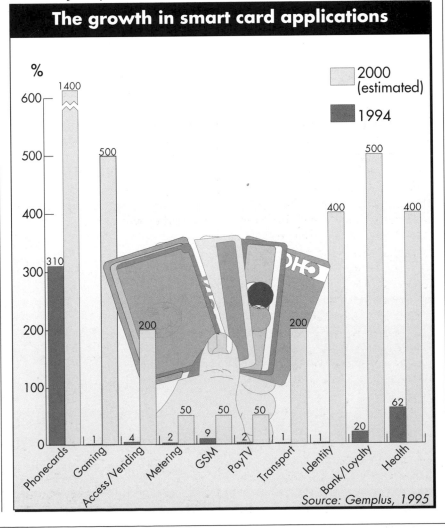

The growth in smart card applications

Legend: 2000 (estimated); 1994

- Phonecards: 1400 (2000), 310 (1994)
- Gaming: 500 (2000), 1 (1994)
- Access/Vending: 200 (2000), 4 (1994)
- Metering: 50 (2000), 2 (1994)
- GSM: 50 (2000), 9 (1994)
- PayTV: 50 (2000), 2 (1994)
- Transport: 200 (2000), 1 (1994)
- Identity: 400 (2000), 1 (1994)
- Bank/Loyalty: 500 (2000), 20 (1994)
- Health: 400 (2000), 62 (1994)

Source: Gemplus, 1995

Identity cards revisited

Information from the Institute for Public Policy Research

The principle of introducing an identity card scheme and whether the time is right for the UK to introduce identity cards

No issue of principle is raised by an individual's choice to carry a document which provides a means of identification. Many of us do so every day. Issues of principle are, however, raised by other aspects of ID card schemes:

- The powers which are granted to officials to stop individuals and ask them to produce their identity card. Such powers may infringe the individual's liberty – the right to be left alone if the person has done nothing wrong – and may lead to discrimination against particular groups of people.

- The information contained on the card, and the databases to which it gives access. The issue of principle here is the infringement of privacy, when officials have access to more personal information about individuals than is strictly necessary for them

to do their job, and the damage which can be done to the *interests* of the individuals concerned.

The question of whether the time is right to introduce identity cards may be rephrased thus: would the benefits to be obtained from such cards, for individuals and society at large, outweigh the dangers, in terms of liberty and privacy, and the costs? We have considered the benefits, such as they are, and conclude that they are minimal. The fact that developments in technology would now enable the Government to introduce a national scheme does not alter the equation: the dangers and costs outweigh the benefits. The time is not right.

Would an identity card be a convenient travel document?

Regular travellers might find some benefit in having a travel document that was smaller than the existing passport. This convenience is, however, outweighed by the disadvantages. Most significantly, if the card were used as a travel

document, UK residents who are not British would, the Green Paper acknowledges, need to have a card of a different colour or be in some other way easily identifiable. This means that, in every transaction where production of an ID card was required, the individuals would be announcing that they were not British, despite the fact that this is irrelevant in almost every aspect of life in Britain. It is known that many people in Britain have negative attitudes towards immigrants and refugees. To require foreign residents to identify themselves as non-British would invite discrimination and act directly against the Government's objective of reducing discrimination and improving race relations.

Would an identity card be useful to provide proof of age?

An ID card would be useful in these circumstances only if retailers were motivated to check the customer's age, or if the penalties for failing to do so were sufficiently severe. It is not in a retailer's commercial interests to ask questions which lead to the customer making the purchase elsewhere. To be effective in preventing young children from purchasing solvents or cigarettes, the cards would have to be issued at an earlier age than those required for other applications.

Would it be useful in banking and retail transactions?

An ID card has a superficial attraction, but there are drawbacks which mean that the security it purports to provide could prove counterproductive. It is acknowledged that, where the incentive is great enough, criminals will obtain the means to produce false ID cards. It will therefore be unwise for banks and retailers to rely on such cards to

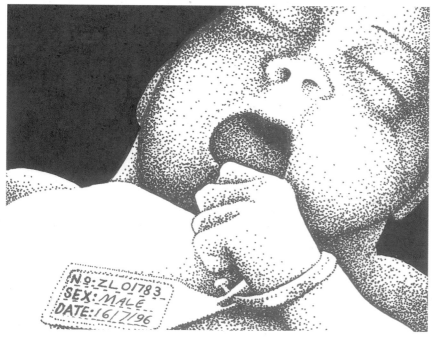

the exclusion of other means of identification. The Association for Payment Clearing Services states that losses from fraud involving credit, bank guarantee and other plastic cards have been cut over the past year by 25 per cent using alternative measures, and additional measures are planned.

Should the card allow the optional addition of emergency medical information or organ donor details?
A national card containing organ donor details is an attractive proposition, given the shortage of donors. But such a scheme does not necessitate a national ID card. There are dangers in having any sensitive medical data on such a card. First, could doctors be certain of the accuracy of the information before relying on it for emergency treatment? If it were computer-readable only, in order to protect the privacy of the individual in everyday transactions, the individual might not have checked the accuracy of the information. Nor would it be accessible to the emergency services unless they carried the necessary equipment to read the cards. Under the Data Protection Act there is provision for special measures to protect sensitive medical information held on databases, but such measures have never been introduced. The public may therefore have cause to fear handing over such information to a central database for ID card purposes.

Would an ID card be useful in preventing crime and the fear of certain crimes?
An ID card is unlikely to make any significant contribution to preventing or detecting crime. It is significant that the Government was unable to cite any evidence that ID cards have made a contribution to tackling crime in those other European countries which have some kind of ID card scheme.

In relation to fear of crime, the introduction of an ID card is unlikely to provide any long-term reassurance. The fact that it is ineffective will quickly become apparent. Published crime statistics are unlikely to fall as a result of this particular measure. The public may then feel that the

inconvenience (e.g. of replacing lost and stolen cards) and the cost (whether to the state or individuals) are not outweighed by any perceived benefits.

Would it be useful in obtaining access to public services and in reducing the opportunity for fraud?
The card could only be of use in obtaining access to all of the services mentioned if it contained a large amount of personal information. The information to which the staff in one service were intended to have access would need to be kept secure so that the staff in a different service had no access to it. Current data protection legislation does not provide adequate safeguards to give the public this assurance.

Secondly, using a single card to obtain access to all services is convenient only until the card is lost or stolen. Some two million plastic cards are lost or stolen each year. If an ID card took a little time to replace, as it is likely to do given the checks which will be necessary before it is issued, individuals will be considerably inconvenienced and thus automatically denied access to a large number of services at once.

● The above is an extract from *Identity Cards revisited*, published by the Institute for Public Policy Research. See page 39 for address details.

© *Institute for Public Policy Research, 1995*

The case for a smart citizen's card for Britain

A summary

1. The development of an electronic Identity Card could provide the stimulus for private sector business to make a dramatic leap forward to an information based society. The implications of this are potentially far greater than combatting crime or streamlining public administration.

2. For this to happen, British commerce and industry needs a single standard Smart Card to maximise the pace and extent of disseminating the new information technologies throughout the economy.

3. A standard Smart Card could best be developed by awarding a franchise to a private operator for a fixed period.

4. Once the concept of a Smart Card became accepted through its voluntary use for electronic payments systems and similar personal applications, it would be possible to apply it for public purposes, such as Identity Cards, Social Security records and tax collection.

5. If Britain took the initiative in developing a voluntary Smart Card for the private sector, she would be well on the way to becoming the world's first Information Society.

6. The introduction of electronic Identity Cards has the potential to cut the cost of public administration, creating the opportunity for lower taxes.

7. The twin achievements of enhancing competitiveness and reducing public expenditure would be a triumphant vindication of Conservative principles and constitute an impressive popular platform for the Government's case for re-election.

● The above is an extract from *On line in time – The case for a smart citizen's card for Britain*, by John Stevens MEP.

© *John Stevens MEP October, 1995*

Identity cards

From The Building Societies Association and the Council of Mortgage Lenders

Would an identity card costing less than a full passport be regarded as a convenient travel document for use within Europe and possibly elsewhere?
It seems unlikely that the cost of an identity card would be sufficiently lower than that of a full passport to make it worthwhile relying on it as a travel document. In time, however, a combined card might be developed, possibly in conjunction with the new-style (i.e. photographic) driving licence. It would be unfortunate, however, if the introduction of a voluntary card, which would be of value to members in terms of verifying customers' identity, were to be jeopardised by being combined with a travel document.

To what extent would an identity card be of added value in providing proof of age?
An identity card would help those who need to prove their age or establish the age of others. However, the benefits of this, in terms of preventing offences such as the sale of age-restricted goods, should not be overstated, since responsibility for requiring production of an identity card, and for refusing to sell goods where satisfactory evidence of age was not provided, would in practice lie with licensees and shopkeepers.

To what extent would an identity card be helpful to individuals in banking and retail transactions?
Members' principal interest in the possible introduction of an identity card would be the extent to which it could assist them to prevent fraud and to fulfil their statutory obligations, under the provisions of the Money Laundering Regulations 1993, to identify new customers. It should not normally be necessary for them to require proof of identity from existing customers in the course of routine transactions.

Council of Mortgage Lenders

Would it be useful to provide space on an identity card to allow the optional addition of emergency medical information or organ donor details?
This might be regarded by some as useful, but should remain as an optional extra.

To what extent would an identity card scheme be seen as a useful way of preventing crime and reducing fear of certain crimes?
Crimes which are most feared are those which involve violence against people or property. An identity card would have little or no impact on current or future levels of such crime. An identity card could, however, play a significant part in reducing 'white collar' crime such as fraud which, though non-violent, nevertheless costs society huge amounts of money every year.

To what extent would an identity card scheme be seen as useful to individuals seeking access to public services and of value in reducing the opportunity for fraud?
An identity card could provide a useful means of ensuring that benefits and services were made available to legitimate claimants, whilst preventing fraudulent abuse of those benefits and services.

What are the implications for privacy and data protection of an identity card scheme?
The simpler the card, the less vulnerable the information held on it and the smaller the danger that the privacy of personal information may be compromised. Whilst technology might exist to 'safeguard' information contained on a card, access to such information will always be available to those who are sufficiently determined.

Should there be a single unique identification number and, if so, should it be incorporated on an identity card?
The incorporation of a single unique identification number could have significant implications for personal privacy and security of confidential information if it facilitated access (whether authorised or not) to a wide variety of databases. A simple card would not need to incorporate such a number.

Should there be an identity card which contained data information about the cardholder in machine readable form and the possibility that this data could be used for biometric checks as a security measure?
There is understandable suspicion that, where information is held only in machine readable form, data could be incorporated in a card without the holder's knowledge.

It would be important that the same information should also be clearly visible to the cardholder (an argument in favour of a simple card, holding a minimum of personal information) or that it should be easy for the cardholder to gain access to a machine reader so that he could find out what information was held. The inclusion of a biometric feature which could be used to authorise use of a card by the legitimate holder could be useful, provided it could be easily verified.

What lessons can be learnt from experience in other countries?
It would be a gross simplification to conclude that, simply because one country refused to adopt national

identity cards some years ago, it would therefore automatically be wrong for the UK to do so now.

Whilst it may be interesting to note the experience of others, the decision as to whether to introduce a card here must be taken on grounds of desirability and public acceptability. In other words, the reasons for the decision taken, whether for or against a card, should be clear and based on a logical assessment of the advantages and disadvantages and not be unduly influenced by what may amount to ill-informed or irrelevant anecdotes.

Is there a case for the introduction of a separate voluntary identity card/travel card?

There is a danger that proposals for a simple identity card could founder if the card were also designed to be used for travel, although the introduction of a simple card need not necessarily preclude its evolution into an optional travel card at a later stage. The key question must be to establish the main purpose of an identity card – is it for verification of identity within a domestic context or verification of nationality and entitlement to travel outside the country of residence? The Government's conclusion on this issue will necessarily affect the nature of any card introduced.

Would a photographic driving licence make a useful de facto identity card?

A photographic driving licence would make a very useful de facto identity card provided the information contained in it was reliable; the Government may therefore wish to consider whether current arrangements for issuing driving licences are sufficiently rigorous to ensure that licences can be relied upon as evidence of true identity.

Is there a case for introducing a dual-function card, in particular one serving the purpose of driving licence and identity card?

It must be emphasised that, if a formal scheme for introducing a dual-function card serving the purpose of both driving licence and identity card is not implemented, the new-style photocard driving licence will be treated as an informal identity card. The implications of this for the security and integrity of the driving licence must be recognised.

What are your views on the possibility, perhaps in the medium or longer term, of introducing a multi-function Government card which would serve as an identity card and could provide extra convenience to the citizen?

The technological feasibility of developing a single multi-function card is not doubted; however, there are inherent dangers in incorporating a variety of highly sensitive information in one card. The potential value of a multi-function card to fraudsters could be immense and could therefore serve to invite far more fraud than a relatively simple card might help to prevent.

What are your views on the possibility of introducing a compulsory identity card scheme based on either a simple or multi-purpose identity card and the level of enforcement necessary?

A compulsory card would be very helpful to members, since a secure common identification system would greatly assist them to verify customers' identity. Given the practical and financial problems likely to be associated with introducing a compulsory scheme, however, the BSA/CML consider that it would be preferable to introduce a card on a voluntary basis. Another argument in favour of this is that anyone intent on criminal activity would be unlikely to observe a statutory requirement to carry a card and some law-abiding citizens would regard such a requirement as unwarranted interference by the State. The fact that a card might exist in such a format as to make carrying it very easy should not affect the right of the individual to choose whether or not to carry it.

© *Council of Mortgage Lenders*
October, 1995

The smart money is on plastic

The 'key to the information age' or a tool for government control of its citizens? By the millennium, credit card-sized computers may be used in everything from a single European currency, to a phone card. John May reports

Smart cards, credit card-sized computers you carry in your pocket, will become almost ubiquitous items in our lives in the next few years. They have been described by one leading research company as 'the consumer or citizen's portable key to the information economy'.

But for all of this, we will pay a price. With plans mooted for cards holding personal medical records and even national ID systems, smart cards will also force a re-evaluation of our attitudes to privacy and data protection.

According to Richard Poynder, Chairman of the Smart Card Club, the professional body for those involved in smart card developments, 'only one application (electronic money) is of real benefit to consumers; all other applications benefit the issuer'.

The heart of the smart card is a chip containing the entire circuitry of a miniature personal computer integrated on to a piece of brittle silicon smaller than a new-born baby's fingernail. The chip is set into a module which in turn is put into a credit card-sized piece of plastic.

The simplest memory-only smart cards can hold 100 times the data held on a normal magnetic stripe card; the more sophisticated can hold many times that, with security features to provide added protection against fraud. This year, the number of smart cards produced is expected to exceed the number of magnetic stripe cards for the first time. Invented in France in 1974, they flourished there, but were considered a national idiosyncrasy and were not popular elsewhere. Now, over 80 per cent of smart cards in use are in Europe. Globally 600 million cards are produced and the market is growing by 30-40 per cent each year.

It is reckoned three billion cards will be in use by 2000.

The spread of such cards throughout Europe will have an effect on:

- The move towards 'electronic' money and the single European currency – banks want to eliminate cash and cut down on fraud.
- The revolution in public transport and the introduction of road-pricing – the transportation sector needs to find faster ways of moving more people.
- Growth of mobile phones – telephone companies see it as a way of cutting overheads and increasing profits.
- Increasing use of information technology in retailing and the future of shopping via television as retailers see it as a way of building data profiles of consumers.
- The whole system of handling medical records.
- Interaction with the various arms of central and local government – democratic governments view it as a way of streamlining bureaucracies, authoritarian ones as a tool for increasing central government control over citizens.

There are 80 smart card projects in Britain at present (set to double over the next three–four years) and 8.5 million smart cards in circulation, predicted to rise to 200–250 million by 2000. The vast majority of these will be for three main applications: phonecards, transport cards and a new type of payment card dubbed the 'electronic purse' (EP). Electronic cash is considered to be the 'killer application' for memory-only smart cards. The 'electronic purse' is designed for low-value purchases in shops and vending machines. It is anonymous, rechargeable and can carry value-added services.

Global credit card fraud is spurring the big three players – Visa, MasterCard and Europay – into switching to smart cards. Most of us will not notice the change but it will

Plastic photocard driving licences

Road Safety Minister Steven Norris announced today that new plastic card driving licences incorporating a photograph of the holder would be introduced in the early part of 1997.

Commenting, Mr Norris said:

'Our preparation for the introduction of these new plastic driving licences is well advanced. The public want them and they will bring significant benefits in terms of establishing identity and the prevention of fraud.

'The process has taken longer than expected, not least because of the need to get the European Union to agree the necessary legislation to allow the new licences to be introduced: the Directive has still not been formally adopted. But we believe that the way is now clear for the introduction of the photocards in the early part of 1997.'

© Department of Transport
June, 1996

have definite advantages, mainly because the cards will be harder to counterfeit.

Smart bank cards have been in general use in France since 1992; the amount of loss due to fraud and stolen cards dropped 25 per cent in the first year of their introduction, and it has been reduced overall from 0.6 to 0.3 per cent. Card fraud in Britain has declined from a high of £165 million in 1990/91 to £83.3 million last year. Forty per cent of card transactions now require on-line authorisation. The introduction of smart cards should accelerate this downward trend.

There are 28 e-cash schemes in operation in Europe, the best known in Britain being Mondex in Swindon, backed by the National Westminster and Midland Banks and BT. Last week Mondex announced it was planning a national roll-out next year.

Having registered for a card at the bank, you charge it up with funds with which you can buy a wide range of products and services, your card being debited as you go. It is simple and convenient for the consumer, the retailer virtually eliminates bank overheads and improves efficiency and the banks gain as they earn interest on the 'float' – the total of the balance in all the issued cards – as well as cutting down the cost of handling cash. The community as a whole wins because of the resultant drop in certain kinds of theft and fraud. If a card is lost or stolen, it can be cancelled and the remaining money credited to the owner.

Visa and the others are also introducing EP cards. The Visa cashcard was unveiled at the Atlanta Olympics. New smart credit cards will also have an EP function allowing the card companies to extend their reach to purchases below the limits for which most debit/credit cards are traditionally used. This will then enable them to customise cards for individual customers while doing very nicely on the additional profits.

A further incentive will be developments on the Internet. Richard Poynder, who was involved with the start of Mondex, thinks it will not be long before many content providers will begin charging for information on the Internet.

The introduction of smart cards could break down the barrier to electronic commerce. Here again the card companies are active. Visa and MasterCard, in discussions with Netscape and Microsoft, have established the standards for secure Web electronic transactions and are working on plans that will enable EPs and credit cards to be used via a 'smart mouse' or other module. Poynder believes 'whoever dominates the Internet market is king'.

The on-line world aside, the most controversy will concern the introduction of smart cards for application in the public sector.

Health cards, for instance, raise many issues, such as how much and what type of information should be stored on the card. Such cards would certainly be a great help for the emergency services and for other front-line health service workers, but the confidentiality of doctor/patient records must be preserved. Who, for example, would own the data on the card, and would governments and insurance companies be able to get access to it? One solution is to have separate directories on the cards, with security 'barriers' between them, thus limiting access only to the appropriate authorities.

Even more controversial are identity cards. The Government's Green Paper on the subject in 1995 suggested smart cards as one option. The research company Demos views the government's planned card as 'an essentially authoritarian instrument' as it gives the citizen no choice about which applications or privacy systems are contained on the card.

It is certain that smart cards will be used for many dealings between the public and public bodies but, at present, there are numerous fragmented schemes rather than a coherent government policy.

Worse, the new technology is not even being used. The new Benefit Payment Card, for instance, launched last month, is a dumb stripe card. At its launch Peter Lilley, Social Security Secretary, said that we have a 'smart system, so we don't need a smart card', although he admitted the system would be able to take smart cards in the future.

Poynder says that Michael Heseltine is pushing for the Government to introduce multi-application public sector cards but that short-termism rules. 'We are reinventing the steam engine with different widths of track for every application,' said Poynder. What's needed, he believes, is a proper national strategy for the introduction of smart cards in all areas. In Spain, he says, 150 banks got together to produce one multi-application card.

They viewed it, he says, like launching a satellite.

But in Britain, most schemes involving retailers are incompatible with different kinds of cards and terminals. Everyone wants to hang on to their own system. The end result may be 'card overload' with so many different kinds of smart card to carry around that we will all need larger wallets. Welcome to the smart card future?

EU poised for 'smart' new driving licence

By Geoff Meade in Brussels

Euro-MPs today approved a 'smart' card Euro driving-licence, despite fears that it could amount to an infringement of civil liberties.

The vote, by 162-114, followed assurances from transport Commissioner Neil Kinnock that a built-in micro-chip would not be used to store information on individuals, 'Big-Brother' style.

The aim is to carry only the licence holder's driving record and possibly medical details in the chip, but even that would require a separate Euro-directive. The licence will be a credit card-sized plastic version to replace paper licences.

It will be pink, with a passport-sized photo and the usual written information – name, date of birth, address, expiry date – in one of the 11 official EU languages.

It will also display the Euro-logo of gold stars on a blue background. Before the vote Brian Simpson, Labour MEP for Cheshire East, warned that motorists would not know the extent of the information stored on the microchip.

He also claimed that the use of a photograph was 'the thin end of the identity-card wedge'. Fellow Labour MEP Mark Watts (Kent East) added: 'There are concerns about civil liberties and I share those concerns but we believe that this proposal builds in the safeguards that are required.'

The new licence has already been welcomed by European Union transport ministers, who will now endorse Parliament's support before returning the plan to Strasbourg for a second and final vote. It is unlikely to suffer a last-minute defeat: the licence is voluntary and will come into force from July next year in those member states which choose to have it.

A Commission statement when Mr Kinnock first announced his proposal attempted to ward off 'Big Brother' scares. 'There is no infringement, potential or otherwise, of civil liberties,' it said.

'The new style driving licence is entirely optional and may not replace or double-up as an official identity card. It is up to any person and/or organisation to decide if they want to consider the licence as a source of information for personal identification.'

One Commission official added: 'There are positive benefits: such a card would not be just a driving licence, but with a chip it could double as a payment card for road tolls.'

The Euro driving licence will be renewable every decade, mainly to ensure that the holder's photograph is up to date. All older styles of licence remain valid and mutually recognisable throughout the EU until their expiry date.

© *Press Association*
November, 1995

On the cards

Privacy, identity and trust in the age of smart technologies

By Perri 6 and Ivan Briscoe

Over the next few years the number and importance of smart cards is set to rise dramatically. Some will be provided by private companies, such as banks and retailers; some by governments using them either as identity cards or to assist in health and social security; others may be provided by non-profit organisations.

Benefits

Such cards offer numerous potential benefits, both for individuals and for organisations. But their introduction raises major challenges to existing data protection law and to our fundamental ideas about privacy. As the flows of data rise relentlessly in the 'information society' of the next century, the questions of how personal control and 'smart privacy' can be created will dominate public policy debates. Smart cards will be the first, the most tangible and the most visible focus for these debates.

So far, however, the debate has been largely polarised between civil libertarians – who tend to oppose any greater use of smart technologies – and those in government and businesses who too often dismiss concerns about misuse of information out of hand.

This book argues that neither position is helpful, and that instead we need a new framework to govern smart cards, and information more generally, to ensure the maximum public benefit from a set of new technologies, and credible guarantees that information will not be misused.

It sets out a strategy for securing reasonable privacy that relies on market-based instruments and the lightest possible regulation. The argument goes as follows.

First, we analyse the factors likely to shape the smart card revolution. We argue that the future of smart cards will be determined by technological developments, the changing and growing patterns of business and government, trends in regulation of the encryption systems used in the cards, and the extent to which consumers trust smart card systems, not least in respecting confidentiality of personal data. In a few years, we can expect on the market single application cards, multi-functional cards issued by consortia of companies and government departments and perhaps multi-functional cards owned by consumers, where consumers decide for themselves which applications they will put on which cards, much as we do today with floppy disks.

Public trust
Second, we examine questions of public trust. Research from the UK and North America suggests that consumers and citizens are at the very least cautious and in some cases suspicious of the implications of the smart card economy for privacy. They fear, first, the accumulation of personal information that lies behind the cards. Secondly, they fear that multi-functional cards could grant some agencies that hold and process personal information – 'data users' – access to personal information not intended for them. At least some government agencies are trusted significantly less than many businesses. A clear hierarchy of personal information emerges that people are increasingly unwilling to hand over, even in return for services.

Policy arguments
Third, we analyse the currently dominant policy arguments. Business, government and technology voices offer reassurance that password, biometric checking, and encryption technologies will ensure more privacy than ever before. Business people often argue that they

have no commercial reason for behaving like Big Brother and that consumers will choose to do business only with companies that respect privacy. They go on to say that the public generally report concerns only about the consequences of loss of cards, not about privacy. Civil libertarians reply that there are reasons to expect a wide and intrusive variety of types of personal information to be stored and accessed from smart cards, and used – sometimes by incorrect inferences – to determine how people are to be treated. They point to commercial reasons why business has an interest in extensive surveillance, in the value of consumer profile information and the market for it, and to traditional governmental tendencies toward authoritarianism. They argue that technology alone will not guarantee security, not least because decryption keys may be traded between companies and government agencies without the knowledge of the consumer or citizen. The only reason that people do not report privacy concerns in market research, they argue, is that they are poorly informed about the risks: when better informed, they become concerned. The market will not automatically select privacy-respecting companies, because consumers do not have sufficient information to choose them, and the mechanism certainly does not work with government.

They document a wide range of abuses, and point to the violations of privacy and the risks of error and mistreatment arising from data matching and data mining, and enforced disclosure of personal information. Smart cards are not a unique source of these evils but they present a new and more frequent source of old risks, and once they are accepted, they will acquire new roles by 'function creep'.

Fourth, we argue that both positions are implausibly extreme. Some civil libertarians may not understand the nature of the new cryptographic techniques, and some seem to conflate arguments about the desirable extent of risk pooling between individuals with arguments about privacy. Nevertheless, there are real risks of abuse. These will be sharpest in the case of multi-functional smart cards.

Government identity cards
Fifth, we show how these debates play out in the case of proposals for government identity cards. The British government has yet to announce whether it will introduce an identity card, and if so, whether it will be a smart card, and whether it would be a multi-functional card for a wide variety of public sector applications, and whether it would be open to business to rent space in the chip for their own applications. The Conservative election manifesto may contain some commitment. Such a multi-functional card would quickly become de facto compulsory, even if neither police nor courts could draw conclusions from anyone's refusal to produce one. It would also

be a major force for centralisation in government, and could represent a quantum step in the levels of surveillance.

Framework of policy goals

Sixth, we set out our framework of policy goals. We argue that the aim of public policy should be to buttress two crucial privacy rights:

- the right to remain anonymous, at least in certain transactions where it is not necessary for the purpose of the transaction to be fulfilled, that the other party knows who one is;
- the right to control the uses others make of personal information they hold about one, that is, to consent to certain uses and to veto certain others.

The present policy regime in Britain does not suffice to secure these rights.

Present policy paradigm

The heart of the present policy paradigm is data protection law, in the form of the 1984 Data Protection Act and legislation to be brought forward shortly to implement the 1995 European Directive. However, the present set of data protection laws are not adequate to control modern data matching and data mining techniques; in some cases are drafted so widely as to be almost unenforceable; provide limited rights for individuals to require deletion and correction; leave action in the hands of the data user or the regulator and not the individual data subject; in most cases provide rights after the event; set up a largely passive system of regulation; provide no support for the use of privacy-enhancing technologies; and have wide exemptions.

We propose to broaden the policy framework for achieving these two key rights, by strengthening data protection law; creating a structurally separate and independent market in data access services as a discipline on data users; creating an ownership regime under which individuals can choose to make up their own multi-functional smart cards by buying blank cards with privacy-respecting architectures from agencies that they trust; promoting the use of privacy-

enhancing technologies; and re-thinking the approach to regulation of strong cryptography.

Data protection law

First, data protection law should be based on the principle that unless the data subject expressly consents to a specific use or disclosure of personal information, that use or disclosure should not be permitted, except in the core functions of government concerned with security and law enforcement. Data subjects should have the right of independent access to their records. We also propose a range of measures to tighten up the present duties and exemptions and to control data matching.

Structural separation law

Second, a structural separation law should be introduced that would create a separate category of data access services. Data user agencies would not be permitted more than small ownership stakes in data access companies, and they would have to allow data access companies the means to provide individuals with accurate and comprehensive views of what is held about them, and, where appropriate, to make corrections and deletions. Even if there is not sufficient demand to sustain many or even any data access companies in the market, the law would provide a discipline analogous to the way that 'contestability' does for monopolists. We set out key principles for implementing structural separation, which are drawn from the experience of cross-media ownership, competition and financial services regulation.

Multi-functional cards

Third, in case the market does not spontaneously offer consumers multi-functional cards over which they have ownership rights, allowing only those applications to co-reside where

they trust the issuing companies and government departments not to abuse the opportunity to 'peek' at each other's data, then government should require that consumer-owned multi-functional cards be made available alongside issuer-owned cards.

Privacy-enhancing technologies

Fourth, if data users (such as hospitals or credit rating agencies) do not use privacy-enhancing technologies which make it possible to guarantee anonymity except where it is absolutely necessary to use someone's real identity, government should take powers to persuade, offer incentives and if necessary to compel them to do so.

Strong cryptography

Fifth, whatever the national security arguments, in our view, there is no point in trying to prohibit private individuals and companies from having access to strong cryptography. However, we argue that there should be regulation to encourage a voluntary system of independent, non-governmental registries that would hold, on a confidential basis, companies' and individuals' crypto-graphic keys; government law enforcement agencies would need a court order to gain access to these keys.

This distinctive five-pronged strategy represents a clear and sensible course, and it avoids errors of the extreme civil libertarian position and the unconvincing bland assurances of some business and technology advocates. We propose light touch market-based instruments of regulation; a clear alternative to the authoritarian vision of a government-issued and owned card as the base of the market; assurance for civil liberties; and a strong platform for business to offer services to consumers that will enhance their lives while also enhancing their privacy.

● The above is an extract from *On the Cards – Privacy, identity and trust in the age of smart technologies*, by Perri 6 and Ivan Briscoe. Published by Demos priced at £9.95. See page 39 for address details.   © Demos
May, 1996

Shops support voluntary ID cards

By John Deane, Home Affairs Correspondent

Bankers and retailers are backing the introduction of voluntary identity cards. They expressed concerns yesterday about the civil liberties implications of a compulsory system, but said a voluntary card would bring significant benefits in combatting fraud and the purchase of alcohol, cigarettes and other goods by under-age shoppers.

Giving evidence to the House of Commons Home Affairs select committee, Elizabeth Stanton Jones, the British Retail Consortium's financial services director, said an identity card would make it easier for retailers to comply with legislation prohibiting the sale of alcohol to those under 18.

It would help to screen for children under 16 trying to buy cigarettes and some solvent-based products, and youngsters trying to buy or rent adult videos. She told MPs that under a voluntary scheme a 'culture change' would be needed, with young people who were at or just over the relevant age limit to buy goods being expected to produce their card in order to prove their age.

Sue Thornhill, assistant director of the British Bankers' Association, said that while on the face of it a compulsory card would be of the greatest value to the banking sector, bankers recognised that 'jumping from nothing to a compulsory card would be unacceptable to the general public'. Mrs Thornhill said: 'They (bankers) do not want to be seen to be shouting from the rooftops that we need a compulsory scheme when they genuinely believe that a voluntary scheme would very quickly gain near universal acceptability.'

Kate Main, Under Secretary of the Council of Mortgage Lenders/Building Societies' Association, said her members were concerned about both the civil liberties implications of a compulsory scheme and its cost – estimated to be at least £600 million.

Both Mrs Thornhill and Miss Main expressed concerns about one of the possibilities raised in last May's Green Paper on identity cards, that a voluntary scheme might be based on a photocard driving licence, which would be issued to non-drivers as an identity document.

Driving licences, even carrying a photograph of the holder, were not necessarily a reliable means of establishing identity, they warned.

Supporters of the concept of a compulsory card have suffered a series of disappointments in recent weeks. First a Home Office consultation exercise found that even among members of the public who wanted to see any kind of card introduced, less than half favoured a compulsory scheme. Then the main police representative bodies told the committee that they too would prefer a voluntary scheme.

Civil liberties groups also opposed a compulsory scheme, as does the Data Protection Registrar, who will appear before the committee next week.

MPs press Government for freedom of information

By Sarah Womack,
Political Correspondent

An influential all-party committee of MPs today called on the Government for the first time to introduce a freedom of information act which would force ministers to justify why their activities should be kept secret.

The report by the committee which scrutinises the work of the parliamentary watchdog, the Ombudsman, said: 'Secrecy can no longer be a solid foundation for the relation between government and the governed. Public trust in government must be matched by Government's trust in the public.'

The MPs' report was swiftly welcomed by the Campaign for Freedom of Information, whose director Maurice Frankel said the introduction of Right to Know laws was now simply a matter of time – 'whether through a change of Government or backbench pressure on ministers'. Labour leader Tony Blair renewed Labour's commitment this week to a Freedom of Information Act. The committee said it was 'convinced that on balance the advantage lies in favour of legislation'. Freedom of information legislation already exists in the United States, Canada, Sweden, Denmark, Norway, France, Australia and New Zealand.

MPs said the benefits of freedom of information were:
- Greater accuracy and objectivity of personal files
- Improved decision-making by ministers and civil servants
- Informed public debate on the issues of the day.

Issues affecting national security and commercial confidentiality would be exempt from disclosure.

The committee was told that Whitehall had put up a series of barriers which were preventing effective use of the new 'open government' code monitored by the parliamentary Ombudsman.

Excessive fees for those requesting data, a ban on the release of documents as opposed to a summary of their contents and a long list of exemptions were cited by Mr Frankel.

But the committee said today that charges should not be used as a form of 'request control' deterring legitimate requests. And MPs complained that the presumption in favour of openness and disclosure had 'yet to permeate' the Whitehall mind. 'The validity of exemptions should be thoroughly considered,' the committee said.

'To scatter excuses like so much gun fire, in the hope that some exemption might hit the target, is to undermine the spirit and purpose of the Code and to show disregard for the rights of the individual requester.'

Mr Frankel said: 'We are delighted a select committee has for the first time ever called for such an Act. The MPs have studied overseas freedom of information laws and found that they lead to better decision making, higher standards of administration and greatly improved public debate, and that the issue is no longer even contentious in countries which have the legislation.

'The time for Britain to have a Freedom of Information Act is long overdue.'

● *Select Committee on the Parliamentary Commissioner for Administration*, second report, Open Government, published by HMSO, £18.00. © *Press Association March, 1996*

Campaign for Freedom of Information

Report on activities 1994-95

Introduction

Much of the Campaign's work over the year has related to the 'open government' code of practice, which commits departments to releasing information on request, subject to certain exemptions. The code falls significantly short of a freedom of information (FOI) act. But it is nevertheless an important development, which should be more widely known about and used.

We have also continued to highlight the problems caused by excessive secrecy across a range of issues and to press for improvements to the public's rights to information, working, as always, with MPs of all parties. We have published briefings, to advise people of their rights to information. Wherever possible – given the limitations of an organisation with a staff of three – we also advise individuals who come to us with problems. And as always we have continued to argue the case for a Freedom of Information Act.

The Open Government code

The *Code of Practice on Access to Government Information*, which promises the release of more official information, came into force in April 1994. The code is not legally enforceable but complaints about non-compliance can be made via an MP to the Parliamentary Ombudsman. While the Ombudsman's recommendations are not legally binding, the government is under considerable pressure to accept them. The Ombudsman has already shown that he is prepared to take a tough line with departments and so far there has been no case of the government failing to accept any of his open government recommendations. On the other hand, if a disclosure could cause significant political embarrass-

ment the government may be tempted to refuse to comply. Significantly, the government has done little to publicise the Code's existence spending only £51,000 on publicity in the first eight months – compared to nearly £2 million spent publicising the Parents Charter in 1991. The Campaign has been telling people about this new right and encouraging them to use the code and complain to the Ombudsman if information is refused.

Testing the code

The Campaign has been testing the code itself by applying for information which has previously been withheld without good reason and challenging refusals.

Our complaints to the Ombudsman have raised issues such as whether ministers told the truth about discussions held with the pharmaceutical industry on disclosure of safety information; whether ministers have – as they claimed – never seen the full report into the economic case for the THORP nuclear plant; whether a report into radioactive pollution in Scotland was redrafted at the Scottish Office's insistence; whether ministers have been advised to say less in Parliament following a legal ruling permitting the courts to rely on Hansard in interpreting legislation; how many files on individuals are held by the security service; and whether the Health and Safety Executive is as it claims legally prohibited from disclosing certain safety information to the public. In some cases the Ombudsman's intervention has led to further disclosures – in others the information is still withheld, or investigations are continuing.

We have also published a

practical guide explaining how the code can be used.

The Campaign has published a survey of the high charges some departments were making under the code – in one exceptional case these amounted to £50 per page! This had substantial press attention – and at least two authorities have since reduced their charges.

We gave evidence on the working of the code, and the case for a Freedom of Information Act, to a Parliamentary select committee.

The Campaign pressed for improvements to a proposed code of practice on access to NHS information. The original draft would have permitted health authorities and trusts to keep secret information which the Department of Health itself would have to disclose under the main code. Following these criticisms significant improvements were made to the final code, which came into force in June 1995.

We called on the government to introduce the separate open government code for local authorities which it proposed in 1993. The local authority associations have resisted such a code and have instead issued a 'good practice note' encouraging councils to introduce their own individual disclosure policies. However, the note itself was significantly improved in light of comments from the Campaign.

New statutory rights

The Campaign has pressed the government to introduce two new legal rights to information, promised two years ago. A new right to health and safety information and a separate right to see non-computerised personal files were both promised in the 1993 'Open Government' white paper, but have not so far been introduced. The Campaign has written to ministers pointing out that the delay is damaging since neither right will apply to information obtained before the law comes into force. The longer the delay, the greater the amount of information that will be permanently excluded from access.

Whistleblowing

The Campaign has helped to draft the Whistleblower Protection Bill, produced with the assistance of Public Concern at Work and introduced by Tony Wright MP in June 1995. It would protect employees and others from victimisation for disclosing information about serious malpractice. To be protected, the individual must not be acting in bad faith; must have tried to deal with the matter internally first, unless it was clear this would be ineffective; and the disclosure must be one that, in an action for breach of confidence, the courts would consider justified in the public interest. The bill would also establish a public interest defence to charges under the Official Secrets Act. We hope the bill will be taken up as a private member's bill in the 1995-96 Parliamentary session.

Crown copyright and the Internet

Anyone connected to the Internet can get on-line access to the laws of America and Australia, to the US Congressional Record and to Australia's Hansard, for the cost of a local UK phone call. However, the equivalent UK information is not available on the Internet. It is covered by Crown and Parliamentary copyright, and HMSO, the government's publishing agency, usually only allows Hansard and the statutes to be published electronically in return for potentially substantial fees and royalties. As a result, Britain's laws are available on-line only from a commercial publisher which charges users $270 *an hour* for access. The Campaign has written to ministers calling for these materials to be put on the Internet free of charge, and warning that the commercialisation of official information will be increased by the government's proposal to privatise HMSO.

The Campaign is itself about to launch its own Internet 'web' site, which will provide information about its work and practical advice on how to use existing rights to information.

Environment

In December 1993 the Campaign published a report revealing that several public authorities with nuclear responsibilities claimed that the Environmental Information Regulations 1992 did not apply to them. We asked ministers to instruct these bodies to comply, but they refused to do so. As a result the Campaign made a formal complaint to the European Commission that the British government had failed to properly implement the European directive on which the regulations are based. The directive requires member states 'to *ensure* that public authorities *are required* to make available information' (our emphasis). The complaint is still being investigated.

Safety

The Health and Safety Commission and Executive have been forced to improve their disclosure policies in two important areas as a result of pressure from the Campaign.

The HSC had argued that it was not fully covered by the Environmental Information Regulations. It would not disclose environmental information about issues such as nuclear safety, because it claimed its responsibilities in these areas were to protect human health, not the environment. Following the Campaign's complaint to the European Com-mission, the HSC accepted that this distinction was unjustified and revised its policy.

Under the 'Open Government' code of practice the HSE had also refused to disclose information obtained from companies prior to April 1994. The Campaign argued that this restriction breached the code itself; the Commission later agreed to drop the restriction.

The Campaign is currently challenging a third HSE disclosure policy. The HSE refuses to disclose certain kinds of information, claiming that a legal restriction in the Health and Safety at Work Act forbids disclosure. The Campaign believes the HSE is free to release it and has complained about the matter to the Parliamentary Ombudsman.

Commercial confidentiality

Information is frequently withheld from Parliament and the public on the grounds that it is 'commercially confidential' – though there sometimes seems little basis for the claim. To try and clarify the issues, we held a seminar on the subject in October 1994, sponsored by the Association of First Division Civil Servants and attended by some 150 people. Topics covered included commercial confidentiality and parliament, environmental protection, prisons and information technology.

FOI awards

Our eleventh annual awards again recognised those who had campaigned for greater openness and authorities which had voluntarily released normally confidential information. They were presented this year by Eithne Fitzgerald, the minister in the Irish government who is drafting Ireland's FOI Bill. Winners included a couple who campaigned for better patient information after their daughter died from drug side-effects; the Chancellor of the Exchequer, for publishing the minutes of his monthly meetings with the Governor of the Bank of England; a small Northern Ireland environmental group which mounted the first successful legal challenge under the Environmental Information Regulations; a Scottish quango for a disclosure policy which rejected 'the fig leaf' of commercial confidentiality; a journalist who

risked imprisonment rather than reveal her sources; two other journalists who have successfully challenged the secrecy of Europe's Council of Ministers; an MP and his research assistant for their sustained campaigning against nuclear secrecy; and the author of a dramatisation of the Scott inquiry.

Media coverage

Our work continued to make an impact on the national media, with Campaign staff appearing on Channel 4 News, Newsnight, Channel 4's Dispatches, BBC 2's 'The State We're In' and radio programmes including Today, File on 4, Radio 5 Live, the Farming Programme and many local radio broadcasts. The Campaign were also consultants to an 'open government' sketch on BBC2 performed by John Cleese and Dawn French. Articles by the Campaign were published in the Guardian, the Independent, the Scotsman, Index on Censorship, Chemistry & Industry and Tribune.

Conferences

The Campaign's staff have spoken at a variety of conferences and seminars including those organised by the Data Protection Registrar;

IBM; the Library Association; the Guild of Editors; the Association of Community Health Councils; the British Computer Society; Liberty; Charter 88; the Directory of Social Change; The House Magazine; the Forum for Interlending; the National Association of Nuclear Free Local Authorities; the Circle of State Librarians; the British Youth Council; a coalition working for a Freedom of Information Act in Ireland; and at a number of schools and universities.

Advice

The Campaign continues to provide advice to many telephone callers and correspondents facing difficulties obtaining their own personal files or information from public bodies.

© *Campaign for Freedom of Information November, 1995*

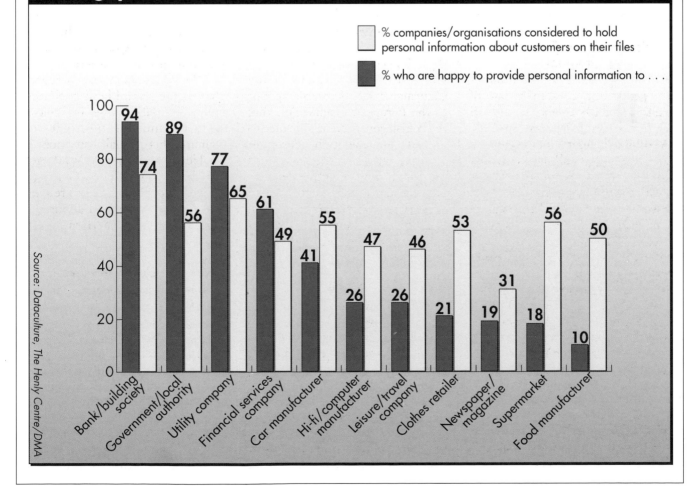

The gap: who has and who could have information about you

☐ % companies/organisations considered to hold personal information about customers on their files

■ % who are happy to provide personal information to . . .

Source: Dataculture, The Henly Centre/DMA

Bank/building society: 94 / 74
Government/local authority: 89 / 56
Utility company: 77 / 65
Financial services company: 61 / 49
Car manufacturer: 41 / 55
Hi-fi/computer manufacturer: 26 / 47
Leisure/travel company: 26 / 46
Clothes retailer: 21 / 53
Newspaper/magazine: 19 / 31
Supermarket: 18 / 56
Food manufacturer: 10 / 50

What is data protection?

An introduction to The Data Protection Act

Why have Data Protection?

The Data Protection Act 1984 grew out of public concern about personal privacy in the face of rapidly developing computer technology. It provides new rights for individuals and demands good computer practice in handling information about people.

The Act also enabled the United Kingdom to ratify the Council of Europe Convention on Data Protection allowing data to flow freely between the United Kingdom and other European countries with similar laws, preventing damage to the economy and international trade which might otherwise have occurred.

What does the Act cover?

The Data Protection Act is administered by the Data Protection Registrar, an independent officer who reports directly to Parliament and in essence, the Act is concerned with 'personal data' which is 'automatically processed'. It works in two ways, giving individuals certain rights whilst requiring those who record and use personal information on computer to be open about that use and to follow sound and proper practices.

Personal data
– is information about living, identifiable individuals. This need not be particularly sensitive information, and can be as little as a name and address.

Automatically processed
– means, broadly speaking, information which is processed by computer. It does not cover information which is held and processed manually, e.g. in ordinary paper files.

To fully understand the Act, you will need to know two further

Data Protection definitions:

Data users
– those who control the contents and use of a collection of personal data. This can be any type of company or organisation, large or small, within the public or private sector. A data user can also be a sole trader, partnership, or an individual. A data user need not necessarily own a computer.

Data subjects
– the individuals to whom the personal data relate.

What does the Act mean to computer users?

Registration
With few exceptions, if you hold or control personal data on computer, you must register with the Data Protection Registrar. Registration is normally for three years and one standard fee is payable to cover this period. Registration forms are available from the Registrar's office, including a special shortened

registration form (DPR4) for those who process personal data only for payroll and bought/sales ledger purposes.

Computer bureaux which process personal data for others or allow data users to process personal data on their computers must also register. Their register entries will contain only their name and address.

Data users and computer bureaux who should register but do not, are committing a criminal offence, as are those operating outside the descriptions contained in their register entries. In these cases the Registrar regularly prosecutes. The penalty for non-registration can be a fine of up to £5,000 plus costs in the Magistrates Courts, or an unlimited fine in the Higher Courts.

The exemptions
In some circumstances it is not necessary to register your use of personal data. However as these 'exemptions' are very narrow and subject to strict conditions, many data users will find it safer to do so.

Registration may not be necessary where personal data are:

1 held in connection only with personal, family or household affairs or for recreational use
2 used only for preparing the text of documents
3 used for calculating wages and pensions, keeping accounts, or keeping records of purchases and sales for accounting purposes only
4 used for distributing articles or information to data subjects
5 held by a sports or recreational club which is not a limited company.

In both 4 and 5 above, data subjects must be asked if they object to the use of their details. If so, the exemption does not apply unless details of those objecting are removed.

If you intend to rely on an exemption you are strongly advised to read 'Guideline 6: The Exemptions', available from the Data Protection Registrar's office.

A *data user's register entry*

A register entry is compiled from the information given in the registration application form. The entry gives the data user's name and address together with broad descriptions of:
– the personal data held
– the purposes for which it is used
– the sources from which the information may be obtained
– the people to whom the information may be disclosed i.e. shown or passed on to
– any overseas countries or territories to which the data may be transferred.

The principles

Once registered, data users must comply with the eight Data Protection Principles of good practice contained within the Act. Broadly these state that personal data must be:

1 obtained and processed fairly and lawfully
2 held only for the lawful purposes described in the data user's register entry
3 used only for those purposes, and disclosed only to those people, described in the register entry
4 adequate, relevant and not excessive in relation to the purpose for which they are held

5 accurate and where necessary, kept up-to-date
6 held no longer than is necessary for the registered purpose
7 accessible to the individual concerned who, where appropriate, has the right to have information about themselves corrected or erased
8 surrounded by proper security.

If the Registrar considers that breaches of the principles have taken place he can take enforcement action against the data user who may in turn, appeal to an independent Data Protection Tribunal. However, if it upholds the Registrar's enforcement action, failure to comply becomes a criminal offence.

What does Data Protection mean to me . . . as an individual?

Subject access

The Data Protection Act allows you to have access to information held about yourself on computer and where appropriate to have it corrected or deleted.

This is known as the 'subject access right' and it means that you are entitled, on making a written request to a data user, to be supplied with a copy of any personal data held about you. The data user may charge a fee of up to £10 for each register entry for supplying this information but in some cases it is supplied free.

Usually your request must be responded to within 40 days. If not, you are entitled to complain to the Registrar or to apply for a court order for access. If personal data are found to be inaccurate you may complain to the Registrar or apply to the Courts for correction or deletion of the data.

Access to the register

The Data Protection register is open to public inspection at the Registrar's office in Wilmslow. Copies of individual register entries are available free of charge (a small fee is payable for certified copies). A register entry only shows what a data user is registered to do, it does not reveal whether or not that data user holds personal information about you.

Complaints to the Registrar

If you consider there has been a breach of one of the Principles (or any other provision of the Act), you are entitled to complain to the Data Protection Registrar. If the Registrar considers the complaint is justified and cannot be resolved informally then he may decide to prosecute or to serve an enforcement notice or notice of refusal of registration on the data user in question.

Compensation

You are entitled to seek compensation through the Courts if damage (not just distress) has been caused by the loss, or unauthorised destruction or disclosure of your personal data. 'Unauthorised' means without the authority of the data user or computer bureau concerned. If damage is proved, then the Court may also order compensation for any associated distress. You may also seek compensation through the Courts for damage caused by inaccurate data.

Further information about your rights as an individual under the Data Protection Act is contained in the leaflet *'If there's a mistake on computer about you'* available free from the Data Protection Registrar's office.

This article is for information only and is not a full explanation of the law on Data Protection.

● More detailed information on the Data Protection Act is contained within the *Data Protection 'Guidelines'* – a series of booklets available free from the Data Protection office. See page 39 for address details.

If there's a mistake on a computer about you . . .

It can affect your life

Today, like it or not, we are all 'data subjects'. Because all sorts of companies and organisations ('data users') have details about us on their computers.

Quite often, this information ('personal data') gets passed on by the original computer user to others.

This growth of computerised records can provide benefits like better medical care, or assistance to the police in fighting crime.

But it also has its dangers.

If the information is entered wrongly, is out of date or is mixed up with someone else's, it can cause problems.

Individuals can be unfairly refused jobs, housing, benefits, credit or a place at college.

They could be overcharged for goods or services.

They could even find themselves arrested in error. Just because there is a mistake on a computer record. Hence the Data Protection Act.

What is the Data Protection Act?

The Data Protection Act gives you the right to see personal data held on computer about you. And more importantly, the right to get it corrected if it is wrong.

In addition, it gives you the right to complain if you don't like the way an organisation is collecting or using computer records about you.

Your rights apply to public sector organisations or private companies which keep information about individuals (children as well as adults) on computer. The Act requires all such organisations to abide by eight Data Protection Principles.

They must:

1 obtain and process the information fairly and lawfully;

2 register the purposes for which they hold it;

3 not use or disclose the information in a way contrary to those purposes;

4 hold only information which is adequate, relevant and not excessive for the purposes;

5 hold only accurate information, and, where necessary, keep it up to date;

6 not hold the information any longer than necessary;

7 when requested, give individuals copies of information about themselves, and where appropriate, correct or erase the information;

8 take appropriate steps to keep the information safe.

A powerful friend

To ensure organisations respect the Principles, the Act also allows for the appointment of an official, the Data Protection Registrar.

Independent of any political or business interests, he has the power under the Act to have inaccurate computer records about you corrected or even deleted.

If an organisation refuses to let you see your computer records, or breaks one of the other Principles, you can complain to the Registrar who can then investigate and help you get things put right.

You may also claim compensation through the courts if you have been damaged by the loss or destruction of personal data, or by an unauthorised disclosure, or even because of inaccuracy.

So, if you think there is a problem, and you would like to see the computer records a particular organisation holds about you, the following sections explain how to go about it.

How can you find out who keeps personal data?

Computer users who keep information about individuals must, by law, appear in the Data Protection Register.

If you are unsure as to whether or not a particular organisation holds such records, ring or write to the Data Protection Registrar.

His staff will be able to tell you:

- if an organisation is registered;
- the sort of information held by that organisation;
- the type of individuals about whom information is held (such as customers or employees);
- in general terms, what the information is used for, where it is obtained from and to whom it is disclosed;

And finally,

- to whom, and where to send your request for information.

However, the Registrar's staff will not be able to tell you whether or not a specific computer user holds information about you.

This you can only discover by writing to the organisation concerned.

Making your request

If you think an organisation may hold details about you on computer, and would like a copy of these, then you should write a letter to that organisation similar to the one opposite. This is known as a Subject Access Request.

If you have not been in touch with the Registrar's office, but are writing to an organisation whose address you already know, then send your letter to the Secretary or Chief Executive.

It is best to send it by recorded delivery, and it is important to keep a copy of the letter and any subsequent correspondence. You are entitled to get a reply to your letter. In many cases you may be asked to fill in an application form, or to provide more details to help identify yourself and to help find information about you. Computer users may also charge up to £10 for providing the information.

The computer user may have divided up the information and covered it by separate entries in the Data Protection Register. In this case you may have to apply separately and pay a separate fee to see each set of information.

However, a computer user will normally explain this in the initial reply to your enquiry.

It will help if you provide the computer user with any necessary details as quickly as you can. You are entitled to receive a reply within 40 days of providing these. You will of course have to pay the fee if required.

If your request is for information about a child, please contact the Registrar to find out how to make such a request.

What will you be sent?

The computer user will send you a copy of the information held about you. The information may be sent as a computer print-out, in a letter or on a form.

However, it must be made understandable, with any codes explained.

What if you don't get a reply or the information given is wrong?

If a computer user does not respond to your request within 40 days or if the information you receive is wrong, you should contact the Data Protection Registrar at the address given at the end of this article.

The Registrar can help ensure you get a reply and, if records about you are incorrect, get any mistakes put right.

If one of the Principles has been broken the Registrar can take enforcement action against the organisation and sometimes may prosecute.

Can you see all the information held about you?

There are a limited number of exemptions to your right to see information held about you. These include information held for the purpose of:

- preventing or detecting crime;
- catching or prosecuting offenders;
- assessing or collecting tax or duty.

However these exemptions only apply if providing the information would hinder these purposes.

In some cases your right to see health and social work details may also be restricted.

If you are unsure or feel information is being withheld incorrectly even in these cases, you should contact the Data Protection Registrar.

Credit reference data

Your right to see credit reference data is covered by the Consumer Credit Act 1974.

A free leaflet ('No Credit?') on this is available from Citizens Advice Bureaux, Consumer Advice Centres, Trading Standards Offices and libraries; or from the Office of Fair Trading, Room Number F306, Field House, 15-25 Bream's Buildings, London, EC4A 1PR.

Your other rights under the Data Protection Act (for example, to have incorrect information amended or deleted) still apply.

If you need further help or information

If you have problems persuading an organisation to let you see your computer records, or suspect that one of the Principles has been broken, or simply require more information about data protection, you should contact the Data Protection Registrar.
Write to:
Information Services
Office of the Data Protection Registrar,
Springfield House, Water Lane,
Wilmslow,
Cheshire SK9 5AX.
Or telephone: (0625) 535777.

© Produced for the Data Protection Registrar by the Central Office of Information

The date

Dear Sir,

I wish to make an application under section 21 of the Data Protection Act 1984. Please supply me with any information which you hold about me to which I am entitled or confirm that none is held.

If you require further information from me or a fee, please let me know as soon as possible.

If you do not normally handle these requests for your organisation, please pass this letter to your Data Protection Officer or other appropriate official.

Yours faithfully,

Regain your privacy

Jenny Simmonds finds 'Big Brother' a little too close for comfort online, but now, with a little care, Internet users can avoid the full force of his glare

A company that tracks the movements of individual Internet users in order to build 'author profiles' on them has begun to issue advice on how users can regain anonymity.

Deja News, which uses a powerful web tool to archive all Usenet postings, has also undertaken to delete the information gathered on authors if asked to do so.

If you have ever posted a message to any of Usenet's 15,000 newsgroups, chances are Deja News has already archived your posting and has started to build a profile of you which can be obtained by any Internet user.

Usenet groups are the 'talking shops' of the Net. Users can post messages and follow the ensuing discussions in 'threads'.

Some angry users decried the company in groups such as alt.privacy, describing it as a 'Big Brother'.

But George Nickas, Deja's media spokesman, defended the company. 'We really have no desire to make people angry at what we are doing,' he said. 'Users are very important to us and we will bend over backwards to help them out.'

Deja News runs on a network of Pentium 133s and other workstations in Austin, Texas. The memory-intensive software was written by the company's founder, Steve Madere.

At the click of a mouse, a Deja News search can vault from individual postings to entire discussion 'threads', from 'author profiles' to Web sites and back again.

I did an author profile search based on my name and was given – in two or three seconds – my e-mail address, the number of articles I had posted since August last year, what percentage were follow-ups to other articles, and what newsgroups my articles were posted to.

Another click would have taken me to the content of each article.

Deja News, a private company, was launched on the Web in May last year (at http://www.dejanews.com/) but did not become prominent until it was added to Netscape's search page in November.

Deja admits to 'dozens' of complaints – about breaches of privacy and copyright – but Nickas said: 'Given that millions of people use Deja News, we think it's a very small fraction who complain. The vast majority of our mail is incredibly supportive. Often a user will flame us on Usenet, but many will rise up and present well-reasoned arguments in our defence.'

So what measures can shy and sly users take against being archived or identified on Deja News?

The company has promised not to archive any posting that contains an X-header reading: X-No-Archive: Yes.

Alternatively, the user can use an anonymous remailer. The best known are anon.twwells and anon.penet. For further information e-mail help@anon.twwells.com and help@anon.penet.fi

Nickas said: 'Anonymous remailers and accounts are good protection. I think there is a lack of perception about just how public posting to Usenet is. If people know what it's all about, and what the risks and benefits are, they can make a more informed choice about whether or not they should participate in Usenet.'

Net porn law faces 'free speech' test

*By Kurt Kleiner,
Washington DC*

Few people disagree that some material circulating on the Internet is unsuitable for children. But a new US law that tries to outlaw such material is being challenged in the courts by universities, civil rights groups and companies. They say that the law infringes the basic right to free speech as enshrined in the US constitution.

Last week a consortium that includes Microsoft, CompuServe and America Online, which all provide Internet services, and groups representing libraries and universities, began proceedings in the District Court in Pittsburgh to overturn the law.

'This case will define the nature and the freedom of information that is available, and will set a critical precedent for how the cyber-community will protect its citizens while safeguarding their freedom,' says Russ Kennedy, vice-president in charge of government affairs at CompuServe.

Last month, President Bill Clinton put his signature to the Telecommunications Act, a huge bundle of new laws dealing with most aspects of electronic communications. Included in the act was the Communications Decency Act, drafted by Senator James Exon. He says that the act is intended to protect children from indecent and pornographic material on the Internet.

Most material on the Internet is not indecent. However, a number of newsgroups and Web sites are devoted to pornographic pictures and writings. But even newsgroups devoted to topics as chaste as the Windows 95 operating system or traditional Irish music often contain foul language when participants lose their tempers.

The law would punish anyone who made indecent material available which minors might see. With nothing to stop children surfing the Net, the law apparently covers every newsgroup and Web site.

The law provoked protests from civil liberties groups, Internet providers and others who argued that it would stifle free expression. In February the American Civil Liberties Union (ACLU) won a temporary injunction preventing the law from being enforced until the court decides whether it is constitutional. Then last week many of the big corporations weighed in with their own lawsuit along the same lines.

'This law is trying to impose Senator Exon's moral code on the rest of the world,' says David Banisar, a lawyer with the Electronic Privacy Information Center, which added its name to the challenge.

Although the Supreme Court has ruled in the past that truly pornographic material can be restricted, the material has to be without any social or artistic merit before it falls into this category. The two suits argue that the law is too broad, and seeks to criminalise material that is merely indecent – for instance, the 'seven dirty words'.

'As a practical matter, it seems to be a standard you couldn't really apply even if you accepted the infringement of First Amendment rights,' says Peter Grenquist, executive director of the Association of American University Presses, which joined in the consortium's lawsuit.

Taken at face value, the law would seem to outlaw a great deal of Western art – for instance the complete works in the Louvre are available online – as well as material that discusses birth control or sex.

A provision of the law does exempt service providers such as CompuServe, and universities which provide Internet access to their students, as long as they can show that they made a reasonable attempt to limit the availability of indecent material on their networks. But Kennedy complains that no one knows what would be considered 'a reasonable attempt'. 'At CompuServe we don't want the responsibility of having to determine what is and is not appropriate for children,' he says. Kennedy says the best way to protect children is for parents to use programs that automatically screen out objectionable material.

The court will hear arguments on the cases at the end of this month.

Freedom for surfers

The Internet is our most democratic medium. Governments should not restrict it

An American court has examined the Internet, compared it to the older mass media – newspapers, radio and television – and found it uniquely valuable. The three judges sitting in Pennsylvania described it 'as the most participatory form of mass speech yet developed'. It represented an ideal, a medium in which there could be a free trade in ideas. The judges spent months listening to expert argument. Their decision spoke in the heightened terms of an historic ruling: 'The Internet is a far more speech-enhancing medium than print, the village green or the mails.' And as it is seamlessly global, the decision affects us. It is our Internet, too.

The court had been asked to protect the freedom of expression guaranteed by the American constitution. The plaintiffs, led by the American Civil Liberties Union, argued that the Communications Decency Act signed into law last February, making it a criminal offence to transmit any 'indecent' or 'patently offensive' material on the Internet, was unconstitutional.

Certainly, sexually explicit material does exist on the Internet, although almost all of it is preceded by warnings. Moreover older laws covering obscenity and child pornography remain fully operative; the US Justice Department has successfully used them recently to prosecute on-line cases. But beyond this, communication on the Internet can be, as the judges noted, unfiltered, unpolished and unconventional, sexually controversial and vulgar – 'in a word, indecent'. It is into this new area that the Communications Decency Act extended the law.

The plaintiffs' objection was that it would prohibit the transmission of some literary, artistic

By Andreas Whittam Smith

and educational material of value to minors as well as adults. For this reason, the new law's opponents included Aids organisations, the Planned Parenthood Association, booksellers' associations, writers' groups, and single-issue pressure groups such as Stop Prisoner Rape and Human Rights Watch.

> *. . .nobody owns, controls or dominates this global web of computers and computer networks, linked together by the world's telephone system*

What did the Court admire so much about the Internet? One feature is that nobody owns, controls

or dominates this global web of computers and computer networks, linked together by the world's telephone system. It is like the roads in this country except that the Internet does not belong to anybody, it exists because the operators of computers and of computer networks in different countries have decided to use a common method or language for transferring data. They have been concerned only with how quickly a packet of data travels around the Internet and not with the content of these missives.

Secondly, the Internet is inexpensive and thus as open to minority interests as to mainstream concerns. For the price of a home computer and a modem linking it to the telephone system, you can connect to and thereby address the world. You could participate, for instance, in the 15,000 or so discussion groups or you could create your own Web site (a Web site comprises material assembled on your computer which any one of the 40

million people using the Internet can call up on to their own computer). Compare this with the effort, time and money required to get a book published, or a newspaper launched or a television service under way.

When challenged, the US government said that providers of material on the Internet which might be unsuitable could take steps, rather as cinemas do, to prevent children reaching it. They might ask 'visitors' to show that they had a credit card, which would rule out minors. Or they could tag doubtful material so that it could be filtered out by special software. The trouble with the first is that the credit card companies would not co-operate in verification unless a commercial transaction is involved. The drawback to the second is that it would be expensive for non-profit organisations to carry out even if the relevant technology existed.

Fortunately, without government prompting, ratings services and software applications are being designed to help parents limit their children's access to the Internet. A Platform for Internet Content Selection or PICS has been launched which provides a positive rating of Web sites. And there is software which will route users to only those sites and no others.

Taking all this into account, the three judges declared the Communications Decency Act unconstitutional. One of the judges said that the Internet may fairly be regarded as a 'never ending world-wide conversation. The Government may not . . .interrupt that conversation.'

Communication on the Internet can be unfiltered, unpolished and unconventional, sexually controversial and vulgar – 'in a word, indecent'

Such a result could not be obtained under Britain's present constitutional arrangements. We have no entrenched right to freedom of expression. A bill similar to the Communications Decency Act could quite easily pass through Parliament and become unchallenged law. While the tradition of free speech in the United Kingdom is deep rooted, in the United States it is sacred. That is why the US Supreme Court could declare 20 years ago that to lose freedom of expression, for even minimal periods of time, 'unquestionably constitutes irreparable injury'.

To arrive at the American level of safeguards we would have to write Article 10 of the European Convention of Human Rights into British law. This states that 'everyone has the right to freedom of expression . . .without interference by public authority and regardless of frontiers'. But it adds that 'this article shall not prevent states from requiring the licensing of broadcasting, television or cinema enterprises'. Newspapers are not on this list of media where special safeguards can be employed. Nor, according to the American court, should the Internet.

© The Independent
June, 1996

Doctors may boycott NHS data network

Doctors are to boycott a huge health computer system because of fear that patients' medical details could be leaked.

The British Medical Association agreed yesterday that until the Government brought in procedures to protect the identity of patients doctors should not sign up to the proposed NHS network, which will eventually link all GP surgeries and hospitals to one data base. It has been designed primarily as a way of passing financial information, but eventually full medical records will be accessible through the system.

The BMA said patient confidentiality was vital, but thousands of

---

Chris Mihill , Medical Correspondent

---

people other than doctors would have access to the data.

Apart from outside hackers, there was a danger unscrupulous health staff could sell embarrassing medical details about people; it was also possible that government agencies such as immigration or the security services would demand access.

Simon Jenkins, chairman of the BMA's information technology committee, said the Government paid lip service to the idea of confidentiality but had resisted the BMA's suggestions on ways to protect it.

Dr Jenkins said legislation was being considered in the US to give insurance companies and others that paid for health care a legal right to inspect computer medical records. Fleur Fisher, head of the BMA's ethics division, warned that if medical records were not protected potential employers, banks, mortgage and insurance .firms and pension companies would seek information.

© The Guardian
June, 1996

INDEX

ADDITIONAL RESOURCES

You might like to contact the following organisations for further information. Due to the increasing cost of postage, many organisations cannot respond to enquiries unless they receive a stamped, addressed envelope.

Campaign for Freedom of Information
88 Old Street
London
EC1V 9AX
Tel: 0171 253 2445
Fax: 0171 608 1279

Aims to eliminate unnecessary official secrecy and to give people legal rights to information which affects their lives. Ask for their publications list.

Charter 88
Exmouth House
3 Pine Street
London
EC1R 0JH
Tel: 0171 833 1988

Runs a campaign on violations of human rights in the UK.

Council of Mortgage Lenders
3 Savill Row
London
W1X 1AF
Tel: 0171 437 0655
Fax: 0171 734 6416

They have published *Identity Cards*, a response to a consultation document published by the Home Office.

Demos
9 Bridewell Place
London
EC4V 6AP
Tel: 0171 353 4479
Fax: 0171 353 4481

Demos is an independent think-tank committed to radical thinking on the long-term problems facing the UK and other advanced industrial societies. They have published *On the Cards: Privacy, identity and trust in the age of smart technologies* by Perri 6 and Ivan Briscoe, ISBN 1 898309 72 8, price £9:95

Home Office
Crime Prevention Unit
Room 583
50 Queen Anne's Gate
London
SW1H 9AT

Publishes *CCTV: Looking after you*, a useful introduction on closed circuit television (CCTV).

Institute for Public Policy Research
30–32 Southampton Street
London
WC2E 7RA
Tel: 0171 470 6100
Fax: 0171 4470 6111

Left of centre think-tank. They have published *Identity cards revisited*, £4.95.

John Stevens MEP
39 St. James's Place
London
SW1A 1NS

Published *On line in time: The case for a smart Citizen's card for Britain*, written by John Stevens MEP and John Worsfold. Free copies are available by writing to the above address.

National Consumers' Council
20 Grovenor Gardens
London
SW1W 0DH
Tel: 0171 730 3469
Fax: 0171 730 0191

A research and policy organisation providing a vigorous and independent voice for domestic consumers in the UK.

National Council for Civil Liberties (Liberty)
21 Tabard Street
London
SE1 4LA
Tel: 0171 403 3888

Defends and extends civil liberties within the United Kingdom.

Office of the Data Protection Registrar
Wycliffe House
Springfield House
Water Lane
Wilmslow
Cheshire
SK9 5AX
Tel: 01625 545 745
Fax: 01625 524510

An independent body responsible for implementation of the Data Protection Act. They publish a student information booklet which provides a useful overview of how the Data Protection Act works. The booklet is available free on request from the above address.

ACKNOWLEDGEMENTS

The publisher is grateful for permission to reproduce the following material.

While every care has been taken to trace and acknowledge copyright, the publisher tenders its apology for any accidental infringement or where copyright has proved untraceable. The publisher would be pleased to come to a suitable arrangement in any such case with the rightful owner.

Chapter One: Prying eyes

Who's snooping on you?, © SHE Magazine, February 1996, *Caught by the long lens of the law*, © The Telegraph plc, London 1995, *Someone to watch over you*, © The Telegraph plc, London 1996, *The Surveillance Society*, © Agenda, June 1995, *Why CCTV?*, © Home Office, *CCTV used to spy on employees*, © People Management, April 1996, *Are you being scanned?*, © Focus, June 1996.

Chapter Two: Identity cards

ID cards – a solution looking for a problem, © Liberty, *The consumer's need for identification*, © National Consumer Council, *Identity cards revisited*, © Institute for Public Policy Research, *The case for a smart citizen's card for Britain*, © John Stevens MEP, October 1995, *Identity cards*, © Council of Mortgage Lenders, October 1995, *The smart money is on plastic*, © The Telegraph plc, London 1996, *Plastic photocard driving licences*, © Department of Transport, 1996, *EU poised for 'smart' new driving licence*, © Press Association, November 1995, *On the Cards*, © Demos, 1995, *Shops support voluntary ID cards*, © Press Association, February 1996.

Chapter Three: Freedom of information

MPs press Government for freedom of information, © Press Association, March 1996, *Campaign for Freedom of Information*, © Campaign for Freedom of Information, November 1995, *What is data protection?*, © The Office of the Data Protection Registrar, *If there's a mistake on a computer about you . . .*, © Data Protection Registrar, *Regain your privacy*, © The Telegraph plc, London 1996, *Net porn law faces 'free speech' test*, © The New Scientist, March 1996, *Freedom for surfers*, © The Independent, June 1996.

Photographs and Illustrations

Pages 1, 8, 10, 21, 25: Ken Pyne, pages 4, 19: Andrew Smith/Folio Collective, pages 14, 16: Anthony Haythornthwaite/Folio Collective, pages 23, 34: Katherine Fleming/Folio Collective.

Craig Donnellan
Cambridge
September, 1996